Wrecks and Reefs!

Wrecks and Reefs!

Shipwrecks and Artificial Reefs
in Southern California
for Sport Fishermen and Divers

Complete with GPS Coordinates!

by Jeff Spira

Published by

Spira International, Inc.
Huntington Beach, California
USA

ISBN No 0–9753524–0–7

Library of Congress Number: 2004092047

first edition

first printing

Printed by:
Hignell Book Printing
Winnipeg, Manitoba, Canada

About the Cover

*The USS Buchanan slips under the waves in the deep water of the Pacific Ocean to it's final resting place. Th
was launched in 1960 in Washington State, and after serving gallantly throughout the Viet Nam and Col
eras, was decomissioned in 1991. On 14 June 2000, the retired warrior was used as a target in a life fire exercis
ship was hit by three Hellfire missiles, three Harpoon missiles and a 2,400-pound laser-guided bomb, but still
sink. A Mark 48 Torpedo shot by a Fast Attack Submarine malfunctioned and missed. The job was finally a
200 pounds of explosive charges set by an underwater demolitions team. U.S. Navy photo by Nick Galante*

For Mari-chan, my sweetie, who makes my life worth living
and my fishing more fun

his book wouldn't have been possible without the assistance of many people.
Special thanks are owed to:

Kay McNamara for her masterful editing job,

John Zolkowski for his support and motivation,

Bill Wilson from the California Wreck Divers, for his
assistance and support,

Joe Liburdi of Liburdi's Scuba Center in Costa Mesa,
for his advice and photos

and for the many organizations and individuals who
contributed valuable information and photographs.

Photograph and Graphic Image Credits

All other Graphics by the author

Important Caution

There are many rules and cautions about fishing near and diving ipwrecks and artificial reefs. First of all, these ships went down for a reason. And more often than not that reason was because the ship proached a dangerous shoal or partially submerged rock, where the ill was torn apart by the undersea obstruction. In approaching these essels by boat, you are likely to run aground on whatever sank the hip originally, so be extremely careful of underwater obstructions as you approach these wrecks. In some cases, you cannot approach within swimming distance of these wrecks in a boat.

ext, the latitudes and longitudes given for the locations of shipwrecks this book are sometimes reported positions, not usually precise GPS rified spots. They are NOT to be used for navigation purposes. Use only current NOAA oceanographic charts for navigation, no matter iat you read in this book or any other source on shipwreck locations. These ships sometimes went down precisely because of errors in ivigation. The writer and publisher of this book do not guarantee the accuracy of any locations offered in this publication. Some of these ecks have moved because of actions of the sea, some have disinte-grated, some are in locations other than where they were reported, and still others, especially many of those that have been beached, ave been salvaged, and the remains have gradually disappeared, buried in the soft sand or mud.

As for those electing to dive in or near shipwrecks, this can be an tremely dangerous business. Diving wrecks is a technical dive, and should only be attempted by those trained and experienced in this tivity. The SCUBA diving certification organizations, PADI and NAUI er two levels of wreck diving ratings, the basic wreck diver for exter-I survey, and an advanced wreck diver rating for wreck penetration, entering submerged wrecks. These require advanced diver ratings a prerequisite. It is essential for anyone considering diving on these ecks, to be properly certified for such a dangerous undertaking. The ter and publisher of this book, will in no way, be responsible for any diving mishaps or accidents. This book is an assembly of publicly vailable information – it does not offer any diving advice or recom-end any activity whatsoever, but merely reports what others have claimed.

Contents

Chapter 1
Secret Fishing Holes

Jigging up and down with a Lucky Joe bait rig, I finally snagged one of the Mack-circling the boat and snapping it up, quickly pinned its mouth with one of the 5/0 bait ⸺ks shut. Sticking the other 5/0 hook of the double hook snell rig through the fleshy ⸺ of the mack's tail, I tossed him overboard and watched as the 12 ounce sinker ⸺ged it down to the structure waiting 250 feet below the surface.

After a few seconds of feeling the mackerel circling the sinker in it's furious but futile ⸺pe dance, WHAM, the Calstar T-90 rod slammed into the rail and remained pinned as ⸺ething major engulfed the mack. I knew I had to get something, even an inch of line, ⸺t the big fish's head just starting to move upward instead of downward. If it had ⸺en the upper hand and managed to take some line, it most certainly would have ⸺ged itself into it's cave and any hope of extraction on my part, would prove to be a ⸺ dream. I strained against the 40 lb mono's resistance to win this initial battle and finally ⸺able to lift the rod to win about an eighth of the 4/0 reel's handle crank's worth of ⸺ Back for another dip, I strained again, this time getting about 6 inches, then back ⸺....

GAFF! I yelled as the big dark shape appeared below the surface after a fifteen ⸺ite struggle coaxing it to the surface. The deck hand took his gaff shot and a 30 plus ⸺d fish came over the rail, to the amazement of onlookers, and into my sack.

Where do you suppose this took place? Halfway down the Baja peninsula miles ⸺ any commercial fishermen? In the sea of Cortez, perhaps? How about when it ⸺ened? Back in the 1930's when fish were plentiful? The 50's maybe? No, on both ⸺ts. This true fish story took place in the mid 1990's on a half day boat, within 20 ⸺tes of the Port of Los Angeles harbor entrance.

This is the kind of action you can find, even today, when fishing the many artific reefs and sunken ships littered across the Southern California ocean. So many anglers w read my web site for the weekly updated fish reports e-mail me with nearly the sa question. It reads something like this: "I have a good boat now, plenty of tackle, a bott meter and a GPS. Where do I find the fish?" Well, this is the book you've been waiting You know the how of fishing, this will tell you the where, exactly where, with G coordinates, to find some of the most consistent and fun year round fishing in South California.

Wrecks and Artificial Reefs

There are literally hundreds of shipwrecks gracing the waters around Southern C fornia. Natural disasters, the movie industry and some intentional sinking of ships produce artificial reefs have all contributed to the littering of the sea floor around coast with the ideal habitat to attract all sorts of native fish. In addition, the Califo Department of Fish and Game has been engaging in an artificial reef program us quarry rock and scrap concrete to create even more habitat. Looking for a place wh fish congregate? Artificial reefs and shipwrecks are the place and here's why:

Toss a rock into the ocean and it falls to the sea floor and is immediately seeded the floating spores of algae, seaweed. This occurs just like if you were to put a pile of in your back yard, it would attract weeds, or if you leave a damp piece of bread on y

counter, it attracts mold spores. Tiny seaweed plants take hold on the rock and start to grow. The crevasses of the rock and leaves of the seaweed provide hiding places for miniscule sea creatures able to rest on their journeys to and from wherever miniscule sea creatures go. With the abundance of tiny creatures, small bait fish find the proximity to the rock a bountiful hunting ground. When these tiny creatures dash out for bits of food, these small bait fish are able to snap them up. With all this eating going on there are plenty of scraps and crumbs falling to the sea floor, so small scavengers are attracted to the rock. Clams, crabs, shrimp, and

Wrecks and Reefs mean kelp, and kelp brings fish, like this sch of Mackerel gracefully circling a stand of giant kelp

ner cleaners of the sea find their way to the rock. With all these shellfish nearby, shellfish
ting fish are attracted to the feast, and with the bait fish in the neighborhood, bait fish
ing predatory fish also pay a visit to the rock to feed off the bounty. Even normally
ts fish species like Halibut and Guitarfish figure out that there are more meals near the
ck than farther away, so they crowd closer. Soon, everything from microscopic diatoms
huge sharks are hanging out at the rock for more protection and better hunting.

That's why reefs are the place to fish - it's simply where the fish are. The more reefs,
ether a sunken barge or a rock pile, the more resident fish. The more resident fish, the
ore spawning and new life is created. The great circle of life and death in the ocean
ntinues.

shing Reefs and Wrecks

Once a submerged reef of wreck is found using a fish finding bottom meter, an-
or upwind of the reef so that the boat drifts back over the reef. Sending live bait or
es right down into the reef or wreck will yield the best results. Such species as Calico
ss, Sheepshead, Perch, Whitefish, Rockfish, Ling Cod, and other reef dwellers abound
r most submerged reefs certain times of the year.

Don't forget the
ges of the reef either.
e flat bottom areas right
acent to reefs and
cks are excellent fish-
spots of flats feeders
e Halibut, Croakers,
lpin and Sand Bass. A
bait or lure worked
und the edges of the
are excellent fishing
tegies to collect these
cies.

Finally, fish the sides,
and areas near the reef
open water hunters like
owtail, Bonito and Bar-
da. Live bait or lures,
ented in a manner to
ce these, are often very
essful tactics, particu-
in the warm summer
ths. Sometimes these

*Jackpot Bob Schiffmacher shows off a beautiful Yellowtail he
hooked while fishing over a prominent shipwreck just off the coast.*

hold deep near the structure, and other times they rise to the surface to chase passing
ools of bait fish who come to the reef to feed, then dash for freedom as they turn
n predator to prey.

In all, work all sides of the reefs, starting with the depths of the reef or wreck itself
including the surrounding flats and mid-water areas above the reef. No action? Fine,

move on to the next. Somewhere there will be action. This is the most consistently go
fishing anywhere in the Southern California ocean and any time of the year.

Diving Wrecks and Reefs

Scuba diving has become an extremely popular sport for many Southern Calif
nians and for visitors to our beautiful ocean. It's only a matter of time before a sp
diver, after a few dives into natural reefs, gets the hankering to explore shipwrecks bel
the surface of the ocean. Well, Southern California's numerous shipwrecks offer all m
ner of wreck diving, from the most basic, to the most treacherous around.

There are old wooden ships that are barely recognizable on the bottom, to ne
complete modern steel ships, and everything in-between including small boats and yac
for the diver to explore. There are deep wrecks, as well as wrecks that are exposed at h
tide. There are wrecks in water with visibility so poor you can barely see your hand in fr
of your face as well as wrecks you can see 100 feet down on the bottom when look
from the surface. Some wrecks can be reached from the beach, while others require m
expeditions.

*You never know what kind of critters you might come face to face with when
diving Wrecks and Reefs*

Chapter 2
Laws Regarding Shipwrecks

The Regulations about the disturbing or removal of any objects or parts of a submerged ship or object are complex and varied depending on the location and age of the
ship. The following are brief synopsis' of the laws, but are by no means, a complete
description of the laws, policies and regulations in effect.

Navy Ships

If you are planning to visit a submerged Navy ship, aircraft or sunken object, here is
Navy's official policy:

> Department of the Navy ship and aircraft wrecks are government
> property in the custody of the U.S. Navy. These seemingly abandoned
> properties remain government-owned until the Navy takes specific for-
> mal action to dispose of them.
>
> Navy custody of its wrecks is based on the property clause of the
> U.S. Constitution and international maritime law and it is consistent with
> Articles 95 and 96 of the Law of the Sea Convention. These laws estab-
> lish that right, title, or ownership of federal property is not lost to the
> government due to the passage of time. Only by congressional action
> can ship and aircraft wrecks be declared abandoned.
>
> Through the sovereign immunity provisions of Admiralty law, the
> Department of the Navy retains custody of all of its naval vessels and
> aircraft, whether lost within U.S., foreign, or international boundaries.
> Past court cases supporting this doctrine include litigation in Hatteras
> Inc., v. the USS Hatteras (1984) and U.S. v. Richard Steinmetz (1992, also
> known as the "Alabama bell case"). The treatment of historic naval air-

craft throughout the world's oceans has also conformed to these laws.

Under the National Historic Preservation Act (NHPA), the U.S. Navy is obligated to protect its historic properties, including ship and aircraft wrecks, for which it has custodial responsibilities. The NHPA directs federal agencies to manage their cultural resource properties in a way that emphasizes preservation and minimizes the impact of undertakings that might adversely affect such properties. It is important to note that the management of Navy cultural resources such as ship and aircraft wrecks is not only a matter of historic preservation. The issues of war graves, unexploded ordnance, and potential military usage of recovered weapons systems must also be addressed in wreck-site management.

The Navy is in the habit of formally abandoning their lost ships. This is done "striking" their ships from their registry of ships. Most of the Navy ships now lying on bottom in Southern California have been striken from the Navy's register, formal act to dispose of them. You may check with the Navy's history web site to determine if a s has been stricken from their register.

The issue of unexploded ordinance is an important one to reinforce. While mechanisms of ordinance devices may deteriorate underwater the potential power of explosive material inside does not. This was demonstrated a few years back when a fish trawler operating out of Coos Bay dredged up a Japanese mine left over from WW Fortunately for the crew of the steel hulled vessel, the magnetically operated mechan had been frozen by corrosion. The Coast Guard lowered the mine into a junk b towed it out to sea and detonated the several hundred pounds of explosives inside wi spectacular pyrotechnic display. Fifty years of rolling around the bottom of the Pac had not affected the power even slightly.

NOAA National Marine Sanctuary

The National Marine Sanctuary surrounds the Channel Islands (San Miguel, Sa Rosa, Santa Cruz, Anacapa, and Santa Barbara) for a distance from the shore to 6 n out to sea, completely surrounding the islands. Here is their policy:

> Except by permit or other special circumstances specified in regulations, the following activities are prohibited within the Channel Islands National Marine Sanctuary: exploring for or producing hydrocarbons, discharging or depositing substances dangerous to the resources, altering or constructing on the seabed, commercial vessel operations within one nautical mile of the islands (except in transporting persons or supplies to the islands), disturbing marine mammals and birds by flying below 1,000 feet, and removing or damaging historical or cultural resources.

Removing or damaging cultural resources, pretty much includes everything shipwreck. Picking up a bronze bolt off the bottom, is included in this activity. nothing, except you may spearfish or hunt shellfish, only in those areas considered (outside the MPAs.)

California State Waters:

Objects within California State waters, that is from the mean high tide line to three [mi]les offshore, come under the state jurisdiction. Any shipwreck more than 50 years old is [co]nsidered "qualified" to be entered into the state registry of historic places, so may not [be] salvaged or disturbed. Sites younger than 50 years old, have no such restriction, how[ev]er, do fall into the category of US Territorial and International Waters.

[US] Territorial and International Waters.

You may only salvage vessels that are abandoned by their owners. Abandonment [mu]st be done formally and in writing. Just the act of leaving a shipwreck on the bottom [to r]ot for a dozen years, for instance, does not constitute legal abandonment. For instance, [if t]he owner of the shipwreck were paid by an insurance company for the value of a ship [and] its cargo, technically, the insurance company still "owns" the ship and has legal claim to [any]thing you may recover.

There's a big controversy brewing among shipwreck divers, scientists, and govern[me]nt about what is best for the shipwrecks - just leave them to deteriorate, or to survey [the]m as underwater archaeological sites, or remove what can be readily taken for display [in] museums, or to be privately salvaged. Rest assured, the sea will eventually claim all [sh]ipwrecks, deteriorating them slowly but surely through the galvanic action of corrosion, [the] feeding off the organic parts of the shipwreck by marine organisms, and the erosion [of s]ea movement. The fact is that if objects from these shipwrecks are not recovered, they [will] disappear forever.

The archeologists claim that all should be surveyed and excavated scientifically. Well, [in C]alifornia, only three permits have been issued to underwater archaeologists to survey [ship]wrecks in the last 10 years. Considering there are over 1600 known shipwrecks in State [wat]ers, it's unlikely that they'll survey even a small fraction of the wrecks before they [disa]ppear completely.

Many divers insist that everything at a shipwreck remain in-place for all divers to [enjo]y. Their logic is if everyone who visited a wreck took a piece with them, eventually [ther]e would be nothing left. Well, that's true, but eventually there will be nothing left [any]way, due to the degradation effects of the sea. What about all the people who aren't [dive]rs? Don't they get a chance to experience these ships of the past?

There's a happy medium here for all. Certainly, historically significant wrecks should [be a]nalyzed and studied scientifically. Popular wrecks in protected areas, like Wreck Alley [in S]an Diego, or the Valiant at Catalina, should be undisturbed for divers to experience [with]out being stripped by visitors. Wrecks like these are also important for academic study [of se]a life and their interaction in an artificial reef environment. Still other wrecks, in the [opin]ion of the author, can be considered junk, and if a diver wants a souvenir, so be it. [Beca]use some drunk fishermen dropped a beer can overboard, doesn't mean that beer [can] on the bottom has any cultural significance whatsoever. Well, when two drunk boaters [coll]ide and their boats sink, does that make those vessels significant?

Most agree that a system should be put in-place to offer something to all concerned, [the s]cientists, the historians, and yes, even the treasure hunters. After all it is only through the [exten]sive investments made by salvagers, that many of these wrecks are ever located at all. [Who] would pour millions of private dollars into years long research studies, high tech sensor intensive sea survey expeditions, and thousands of man-hours underwater, a there's no chance to recover even a part of the investment? No one. That's why even th search for lost shipwrecks will cease if only governmental agencies are in control of th finds, or possibly the searches will go underground, without the knowlege of the scientis That would be a great loss for those interested in keeping this history alive.

One thing to keep in mind, though. When ships or boats sink, often people d These shipwrecks may be the only gravestones the lost lives will ever have. Keep that mind when you're exploring these vessels. These wrecks can house the legacies of bra men fighting to save their ships, long forgotten tales of the sea, and the forgotten histor of people's lives.

Chapter 3
Santa Barbara & Ventura Counties

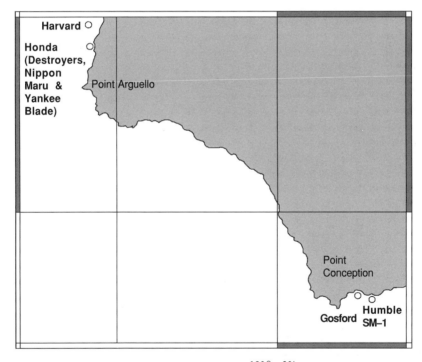

The Santa Barbara and Ventura county coastlines, while having no artificial reefs, are
endowed with natural reefs for the fisherman. In addition quite a number of very
profile wrecks are in the area, especially in the Point Arguello area. The point area is a
way from any port and is famous for its poor weather, foggy conditions, rough seas,
urrents, and rocky coastline - in other words, a generally very dangerous place for
ation. For those with plenty of experience and a willingness to wait for nice weather
vater conditions, it represents a fascinating historical perspective and some of the
productive fishing in the entire state. Just some of the major wrecks are described

The Harvard

In 1931, a 400 foot long passenger steamship, the Harvard, ran aground on so rocks just North of Point Arguello, in heavy fog. When it was built in 1907, it was cons ered the fastest passenger ship afloat and made a number of transatlantic journeys bri ing Irish immigrants from their homeland to New York. In the 1920s, it found itself in Pacific shuttling passengers between San Francisco and Los Angeles, until it's date w destiny in the fog in 1931. The Harvard lies at:

34° 36.933'N x 120° 38.833'W

Like most of the Point Arguello wrecks, the Harvard is in very rocky, tricky navigate water with treacherous currents, frequent storms, limited visibility and in-gene very foul water to attempt to navigate. There are days, though, when the sea is beaut and mild and at those times, the wreck is fishable, with plentiful rockfish on tap awai the diligent fisherman lucky enough to find himself in the right place at the right time

The Great Destroyer Tragedy of 1923

It was back in 1923 when seven US Navy destroyers were on their way south f San Francisco to Long Beach after a high speed shakedown cruise, when the lead stroyer, the Delphy (DD-261) turned to the East from their Southerly course hea down the central California coast. The turn was supposed to have taken the lead ship : Point Conception and into the East-West running Santa Barbara channel separating Santa Barbara coastline from the string of islands known as the Northern Channel Isla Unfortunately that was before the advent of navigational electronics and with the wor ing weather that day, errors in dead reckoning put the ships more than eight miles N of where the captain thought they were. Shortly after the turn, the Delphy plowed inte rocks at Point Arguello, known as Honda, or the Devils Jaw.

Back then, with no radars, ships in poor visibility conditions steered by following the wake of the ship in front of them, so one after another, the next six ships followed the Delphy into the shallow water reefs to be broken open on the sharp rocks of the coastline and

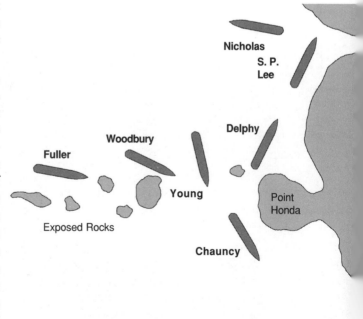

Positions of the ships at the site of the calamity

it to their watery graves. When it was all over, seven ships, the Delphy (DD-261), the auncy II, (DD-296), the Fuller (DD-297), the Woodbury III (DD-309), the S. P. Lee D-310), the Nicholas (DD-311), the Young (DD-312) were destroyed and 23 lives re lost in the tragedy. Fortunately, several other destroyers following in the convoy

The USS Delphy, DD-261, one of the prides of the US Navy in the 1920s

red out what was happening and averted disaster.

The ships lie in fairly shallow water in the midst of a number of boiler rocks. They've 1 dived on over the years and partially salvaged, but there's plenty of wreckage there his day to provide a substantial fish habitat. The ship positions are shown in the draw-Extreme caution should be exercised in this area since the water currents are treacher-and numerous boiler rocks are just submerged enough to evade detection in calmer r are waiting to do to your boat what they did to the pride of the Navy back in 1923.

The scene of the tragedy

Occasionally the water flattens out, though, and the fishing turns fantastic. The horri
weather of the area, plus it's distance from any port, more than 30 miles from either Sa
Barbara or Port San Luis, makes it a very seldom fished area. Shallow water rock f
abound in the area, as do Halibut, Rock Sole, Cabezon, and a number of other species.
certain times of the year, Ling Cod and White Seabass are also possible here.

Diving the Honda destroyers is not for the inexperienced and never a predicta
thing. The weather in this area means the surges and currents are severe. Only the calm
of days are suitable for diving on these wrecks. There are the occasional days, thou
when the seas and currents subside and the patient diver is rewarded with the experie
of a lifetime. Early destroyers, like these seven, were covered in amazing brass and bro
fittings. Though much of it has been salvaged over the years, the sea floor is still litte
with fascinating artifacts. Beware of unstable ordinance in this area. Don't hit unkno
objects with hammers.

The Nippon Maru

At the identical site as the Great Destroyer Tragedy of 1923, a mere ten years late
1933, a 400 foot long Japanese Naval tanker made the same fatal mistake as the c
mander of the Delphy. Thinking he'd passed Point Conception and Arguello in the
the Captain turned to steam down the Santa Barbara Channel. The sharp rocks of p
Honda were no less efficient at slicing his ship open than they were with the destroy
and sent the big tanker to the bottom. It lies in 70 feet of water at:

34° 36.133'N x 120° 38.833'W

Like the Honda destroyers, the area the Nippon Maru sits in is difficult and tre
erous. See the Honda destroyer description for fishing and diving information.

The Yankee Blade

The Yankee Blade is a 1700 ton, 263 foot long side wheel steamship that sunk ne
Point Pedernales in 1854. It was in a race against another ship, the Sonora at the time. S
always possible that the competetive spirit of the crew contributed to a relaxing o
caution that is always a part of safe seamanship. The Yankee Blade became famou
cause it was carrying a load of gold bullion from the gold rush mining operatio
Northern California along with 812 passengers and a crew of 122. Much of the shi
been scavenged over the years but the machinery is still scattered along the bottom. Wh
all of the gold has been recovered is a topic of considerable debate, but rest assured
treasure seekers have at least taken a look to see if they could become rich and fam

The Yankee Blade sits in an area of the coastline known for its rough swell:
treacherous currents. It is offshore from Vandenburg Air Force Base and sits in 75 f
water on a hard bottom at:

34° 36.133' N x 120° 38.733' W

Like the destroyers and the Nippon Maru, fishing or diving the Yankee Blade

The Yankee Blade is a sidewheel steamship very similar to this Navy sidewheeler, the Mississippi built about the same time

the faint of heart, nor for those without substantial experience and a good boat.

sford

The Gosford is a 2200 ton steel hulled sailing ship that caught fire in 1893, was ially beached, and then sank and partially slid into deeper water off Government Point he western Santa Barbara county coastline. This ship lies in a well protected area on a y bottom. It normally grows a healthy stand of kelp, but occasional storms wipe the free. It's in 20 to 40 feet of water at:

34° 27.000'N 120° 26.333'W

Fishing the Gosford is like fishing any other kelp bed. Calico Bass, White Seabass, when the weather is fair, Barracuda and Bonito visit the surface and mid water areas. Bass, Sheepshead, and Sculpin ply the bottom. Surrounding the wreck Halibut and r flats species can be found in abundant numbers.

Divers will find the Gosford difficult to distinguish from a natural reef since it often s healthy stands of kelp. Occasionally, during El Niño years or after storms, the kelp pears and the remains of the hull can be more easily discerned. Of the many wrecks uthern California, this one can be disappointing to the diver because it lacks many rnable features, except for the prominant bowsprit. Nonetheless, diving on any wreck experience not soon forgotten.

ble SM-1

Originally a WWII Navy landing craft, the Humble SM-1 drilling ship was built in 'edro, California and comissioned as the LSM-251 (Landing Ship, Medium, #251) in It was decomissioned after the war in 1947 and donated to the Port Authority of

Newport, Oregon who later sold the ship to the Humble Oil and Refining Compa[ny]. Humble Oil converted it to a drilling ship, arguably the first of its kind, in 1956, a[nd] named it the SM-1. It was anchored in the Santa Barbara Channel between the Chan[nel] Islands and the coastline when, in 1961, during a storm, the ship took on too much wa[ter] and sank. It lies in about 80 feet of water in the channel at:

$$34° \ 26.833' \ N \ x \ 120° \ 25.667' \ W$$

The LSM-257, sistership to the Humble SM-1 (LSM-251) doing its duty during WWII in the Pacific theater of the war.

The ship sits on a hard bottom, so it gets its share of flats fish surrounding [the] wreck, Sand Bass, Halibut, Sculpin, Cabezon, and occasionally Rock Sole are the [usual] visitors to the site. In addition, clouds of perch inhabit the wreck along with the occas[ional] bigger predatory fish.

For the diver, the SM-1 is a technically difficult dive. The currents here tend t[o be] quite strong, so maintaining your position is sometimes, difficult. The ship lies up[side] down on the bottom and the only way in is through the drilling hole. This is an extre[mely] dangerous wreck to enter for all but the most experienced wreck divers. Many d[ivers] report becoming very disoriented after entering the wreck since it is upside down. [That] being said, it is a strong lure for those interested in visiting this famous vessel.

Jenelle

The La Jenelle was a [pas]senger liner built in [19]9. It was 465 feet long [and] displaced 12,500 tons. [In] eh beginning, the ship [was] named the Bahama [Star] and was used as an [earl]y cruise ship out of [Mia]mi. In those days, only [the] wealthy could afford [ocea]n trips for fun, rather [tha]n for transportation [us]e, so the ships and their [interi]ors were elegant and [lux]rious.

When WWII broke [out,] the Bahama Star was [presed] into service by the [US] Navy, like most pas[seng]er ships in US waters [at th]e time. In war, the [Bah]ama Star was shot at [by] naval gunfire and [torp]edoes alike, always [mana]ing to come through [unsc]athed. Crewmembers [and] passengers started calling it the Lucky Star.

Seals and Sea Lions, like this Harbor Seal, are frequent companions to Reef and Wreck divers

After the war, the Bahama Star was returned to its owners and resumed its duties of [carry]ing wealthy tourists around the Carribean until the 1960s. In 1959, there was a terrible [fire] aboard the cruise ship Yarmouth Castle. One hundred sixty five people were killed, [result]ting in totally new safety regulations for all passenger carrying ships in the US. The [oper]ators of the Bahama Star pulled it out of service in 1968 when it was decided that the [cost] of making the required alterations of an old ship were prohibitive, so a new ship [woul]d be purchased to resume the route.

The Bahama Star was sold in 1968 and the new owners renamed it La Jenelle. It was [towed] through the Panama Canal to Port Hueneme, and anchored there. The ship then [passe]d through several hands, each owner unable to follow through in putting the proud [ship] back in service. It just sat there at anchor, swinging around with each shift of the [wind]s and tide.

On April 13th, 1970, a howling storm hit the Santa Barbara Channel with 65 miles [per h]our winds, 10 to 12 foot seas and driving rain. The pounding seas and wind dragged [the an]chor of the ship and slammed it into the beach just off the Port Hueneme breakwa-[ter. T]he grounding left holes in the bottom and seawater poured in. Two men were

aboard, desperately pumping out the bilges, but they soon realized their efforts w
hopeless, so decided to abandon ship. A Navy helicopter finally plucked the two off
bridge of the ship as it wallowed and rolled on its side and the pounding seas brok
apart.

Today, pieces of the La Jenelle remain a part of the Port Hueneme breakwa
while others serve as an of artificial reef attracting fish very near to the entrance to 1
Hueneme's busy port. The two most prominant pieces of the wreckage lie at:

34° 08.093'   119° 17.731'
34° 07.743'   119° 17.784'

The La Jenelle site is now a popular fishing spot. It attracts Perch, Bass, and sha'
water Rockfish. In addition, flats fish like Halibut, Sand Bass and Sculpin are attracte
the area in-season. In the warmer months, Barracuda and sometimes Bonito visit the wreck to sample the buffet of prey often using the reef for cover.

As for diving, the La Jenelle is one of the few Southern California wreck dives acessible from the beach. Though the visibility is usually fairly poor, on calmer days it improves considerably and there is much to explore of this once huge ship.

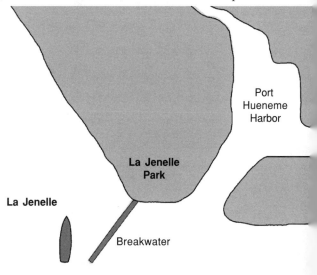

La Jenelle's final resting place relative to the Port Hueneme Breakwater. A park now commemorates the great ship's demise.

Additional Santa Barbara and Ventura County Wrecks

Following are some additional shipwrecks from California's Shipwreck dat
There is no guarantee that anything remains of these shipwrecks, many have bee:
vaged, buried, or simply disappeared by the action of the sea. Also, there is little assu
that the coordinates are even correct. They are simply the reported positions of w
The majority of these wrecks went down before the days of the Global Positi
System and Loran, and often errors in Navigation were the very reasons these vessels
destroyed in the first place.

The Santa Barbara and Ventura County wreck charts are organized from Sou
North by wreck location.

Santa Barbara County

Name	Type	Sunk	Reason	Tons	Coordinates	
ion Planet		1955			34° 20.00' N	119° 40.00' W
cretia K	Oil screw	1958		54	34° 20.00' N	119° 48.00' W
orgina	Gas screw	1931		38	34° 22.00' N	119° 29.00' W
iple Crown	Supply boat	1968			34° 22.50' N	119° 40.00' W
zabeth		1847			34° 23.00' N	119° 42.50' W
cky Star		1950			34° 23.00' N	119° 41.00' W
solute	Oil screw	1952		90	34° 23.00' N	120° 20.00' W
ura Bevin		1857			34° 23.50' N	119° 42.00' W
llulah		1955			34° 24.00' N	119° 50.00' W
a Lion	Oil screw	1954	Burned	89	34° 24.67' N	120° 26.50' W
andard		1936	Wrecked		34° 24.75' N	119° 41.00' W
n Juan		1943	Wrecked		34° 24.75' N	119° 41.00' W
tta		1868	Wrecked		34° 24.75' N	119° 41.00' W
ancisca	Brig	1847	Stranded		34° 24.75' N	119° 41.00' W
tril	Sloop	1902	Storm		34° 24.75' N	119° 41.00' W
nlight		1932	Wrecked		34° 24.75' N	119° 41.00' W
za Thornton		1856	Stranded		34° 24.75' N	119° 41.00' W
de of the Sea					34° 24.75' N	119° 41.00' W
w Life		1932	Wrecked		34° 24.75' N	119° 41.00' W
nwan	Oil yawl	1943	Foundered	219	34° 24.75' N	119° 41.00' W
rland	Fishing boat				34° 24.75' N	119° 41.00' W
zzani		1856	Wrecked		34° 24.75' N	119° 41.00' W
mboldt	Drill ship				34° 25.00' N	120° 22.00' W
etco	Schooner	1918	Burned	103	34° 25.17' N	119° 36.00' W
lma Kelley	Oil screw	1949			34° 26.00' N	120° 26.00' W
asta	Steam schooner	1906	Grounded	722	34° 26.50' N	120° 27.17' W
n Pedro	Steam scow	1894			34° 26.67' N	120° 26.00' W
mble SM-1	Drilling barge	1961	Foundered	735	34° 26.83' N	120° 25.67' W
us		1921	Wrecked		34° 26.83' N	119° 28.33' W
eida Victory	Victory ship	1946			34° 26.83' N	120° 28.17' W
R Emmet		1946			34° 26.92' N	120° 28.33' W
van		1941			34° 26.92' N	120° 28.25' W
omas Crowley		1921			34° 26.92' N	120° 28.33' W
ecrans	Oil steamer				34° 27.00' N	120° 08.00' W
keley	Steam schooner	1907	Burned	571	34° 27.00' N	120° 29.00' W
sford	steel hulled Bark	1893	fire and beaching	2251	34° 27.00' N	120° 26.33' W
ibus	Gas screw	1924			34° 28.00' N	120° 13.00' W
llis	Oil screw	1952	Burned	82	34° 28.00' N	120° 13.00' W
T & B Co #6	Scow	1931	Wrecked	738	34° 28.00' N	120° 13.00' W
na	Schooner	1846	Stranded		34° 28.06' N	120° 12.07' W
halis	Steam schooner	1933	Collision	663	34° 28.17' N	120° 28.00' W
ign	Schooner	1909	Stranded	618	34° 28.33' N	120° 13.08' W
ch	Steam screw	1849	Grounded	400	34° 30.00' N	120° 35.00' W
Loggie	Steam schooner	1912	Grounded	404	34° 33.92' N	120° 38.33' W
ifred O'Donnell		1927			34° 34.60' N	120° 39.00' W
Kulukundis	Liberty ship	1949	Stranded		34° 34.60' N	120° 39.00' W
e Eagle		1940	Wrecked		34° 34.60' N	120° 39.00' W
Angeles	Dredge	1942	Wrecked	199	34° 34.60' N	120° 39.00' W
mi	Racing yacht	1955	Collision		34° 34.60' N	120° 39.00' W
on Maru	naval tanker	1933	grounded in fog	5842	34° 36.13' N	120° 38.83' W
kee Blade	Sidewheel Steam	1854	Grounded	1767	34° 36.13' N	120° 38.73' W
hi	Destroyer	1923	Stranded	1250	34° 36.17' N	120° 38.83' W
Lee	Destroyer	1923	Stranded	1250	34° 36.17' N	120° 38.83' W
uncy	Destroyer	1923	Stranded	1250	34° 36.17' N	120° 38.75' W
er	Destroyer	1923	Stranded	1250	34° 36.17' N	120° 38.83' W
ng	Destroyer	1923	Stranded	1250	34° 36.17' N	120° 38.83' W

17

Santa Barbara County (cont.)

Name	Type	Sunk	Reason	Tons	Coordinates
Woodbury	Destroyer	1923	Stranded	1250	34° 36.17' N 120° 38.83'
Nicholas	Destroyer	1923	Stranded	1250	34° 36.17' N 120° 38.83'
Yankee Mariner	Oil screw	1949	Burned	363	34° 36.20' N 120° 39.00'
Santa Rosa	Steam screw	1911	Grounded	2416	34° 36.50' N 120° 38.20'
Harvard	Steam liner	1931	Grounded	3737	34° 36.93' N 120° 38.83'
Sibyl Marston	Steam screw	1909	Stranded	1086	34° 40.33' N 120° 36.58'
El Commodore	Oil screw	1946	Stranded	117	34° 41.00' N 120° 36.42'
Robert Sudden	Bark	1905	Wrecked	616	34° 41.00' N 120° 36.42'
Hopestill	Oil screw	1949	Stranded		34° 45.42' N 120° 38.17'
Scotia	Steam screw	1914	Stranded	181	34° 45.42' N 120° 38.17'
Crovate		1923	Wrecked		34° 54.10' N 120° 40.42'
Annie Lysle	Schooner	1875	Stranded		34° 54.10' N 120° 40.42'

Ventura County

Name	Type	Sunk	Reason	Tons	Coordinates
Andrew D	Oil screw	1953	Burned	116	33° 45.00' N 118° 50.00'
Sea Products #1	Barge	1927	Foundered	57	33° 58.00' N 118° 48.00'
Saint Croix	Steamship	1909	Burned	1993	34° 00.00' N 118° 45.00'
Humanity		1939	Wrecked		34° 00.00' N 118° 48.00'
Spray	Fishing boat	1939	Capsized		34° 05.00' N 119° 03.58'
R C Co #2	Scow	1939	Stranded	402	34° 07.27' N 119° 09.80'
Caeser Burns	Schooner	1889			34° 08.00' N 119° 13.00'
Sitka		1934			34° 08.00' N 119° 13.00'
La Jenelle	Steam screw	1970		7000	34° 08.67' N 119° 12.83'
Kopco Star	Oil screw	1963		60	34° 08.75' N 119° 12.00'
Yaquina	Screw	1897	Wrecked		34° 09.00' N 119° 12.50'
Aloah		1952			34° 09.00' N 119° 12.50
Caroline E Foote		1871			34° 09.00' N 119° 12.50
Chris C	Oil screw	1937	Foundered	60	34° 09.00' N 119° 12.50'
Portland	Barkentine	1906		493	34° 09.00' N 119° 14.00
Linde	Oil screw	1951	Stranded	73	34° 09.00' N 119° 14.50'
California		1883			34° 09.20' N 119° 13.25
Pal	Oil screw	1937	Wrecked	71	34° 13.37' N 119° 15.67
Unknown	many wrecks				34° 14.00' N 119° 16.00'
Coos Bay	Steam screw	1914	Wrecked	544	34° 14.00' N 119° 16.00
W L Hardison	Steamship	1889	Burned		34° 16.00' N 119° 17.50
Crimea	Brig	1876	Stranded		34° 16.33' N 119° 17.50
Advance	Brig	1870	Wrecked	210	34° 16.33' N 119° 17.50
Lucy Ann	Brig	1875	Stranded		34° 16.40' N 119° 17.17
Kalorama	Steam schooner	1876			34° 16.42' N 119° 17.50
Gualala	Schooner	1888	Stranded		34° 16.50' N 119° 17.50
Sonoma	Oil screw	1949	Foundered	196	34° 16.50' N 119° 17.50
James Higgins		1916			34° 16.80' N 119° 16.80
G Marconi	Oil screw	1931	Burned	100	34° 20.00' N 120° 40.00
Saint Paul	Steam screw	1905	Stranded	2440	34° 20.42' N 119° 26.12
McCulloch	Cutter	1917	Collision		34° 29.30' N 120° 29.50

California Sheepshead peeks out from its territory staked out in a shipwreck. Protection from predators and a nearby food supply are two of the reasons fish seek out and inhabit shipwrecks and artificial reefs

Fabulous Gorgonians are a common sight when diving on shipwrecks and artificial reefs

Chapter 4
Northern Channel Islands

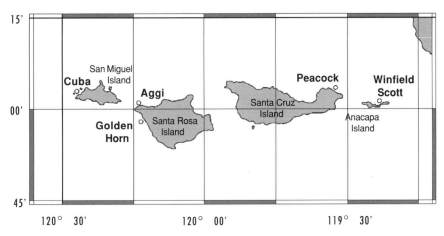

The Northern Channel Islands consist of a string of rocky islands oriented in an
_vest direction, about 25 miles off the Santa Barbara coastline. Though these islands
been owned privately and by the US Government (Department of the Navy) over
ears, they're now converting to a National Park. They're named (from West to East)
viiguel Island, Santa Rosa Island, Santa Cruz Island, and finally, Anacapa Island, the
est and farthest East of the islands.

The Northern Channel Islands are fascinating places with a wide variety of land
als, sea life, geographical features and important archeological and paleological sites.
and ranges from rocky cliffs to wide grasslands and the coastlines feature rocky reefs,
beaches and cavernous grottos opening into the sea. There are few pristine places
ning along the California Coast and the Channel Islands represent a clear look back
he history of the California Coast before the advent of homes, freeways, factories
he infrastructure of modern life.

Up-to-date information about the Northern Channel Islands may be obtained through

the Channel Islands National Park web site at www.channel.islands.national-park.cc
Camping, boating and activity calenders are on-line and brochures, maps and other visi
information are available through the web site.

The Northern Channel Islands provide excellent fishing all year round, with ev
type of marine habitat imaginable, shallow reefs, deep reefs, mud flats, sandy bottc
and blue water. The establishment of artificial reefs here would be redundant with
abundance of natural structures for the local fish to inhabit. However, the rocky isla
can be hazardous for boats and a number of shipwrecks in the area offer the fisherr
specific opportunities for wreck fishing. Many of these wrecks are from strandings,
they are in shallow water and are popular with divers. Several worth investigating for
fishermen are included herein.

Certain sections of the Channel Islands have been delegated MPAs, Marine I
tected Areas. In these areas there is no fishing or taking of any biological, geologica
cultural item. Even picking up a seashell off the bottom constitutes a crime. You :
boat, anchor or dive in these areas, but do not disturb anything you may see. The M
for the Northern Channel Islands are shown below:

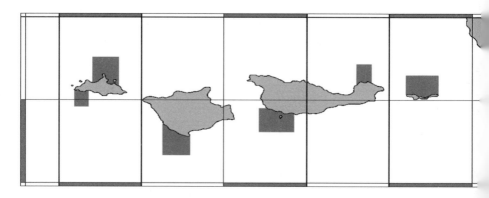

The MPAs - Consult the California Department of Fish and Game web site: http://www.dfg.gov
for precise MPA borders and regulations.

In additon to the MPAs, the Channel Islands have been identified as a Nati
Marine Sanctuary. This extends 6 miles from the shorelines of the Islands (not the I
areas, the entire Islands) and within this boundary, no cultural, archeological or palentolo
artifact may be disturbed, except by permit - so you may not take anything you might
at a shipwreck site.

Cuba

The steamship Cuba was originally built in Germany in 1897 by the famous
man shipyard Blohm and Voss, the very same shipyard that built the battleship Bisr
The ship was originally named the Coblenz. It was an extremely well built ship and fc
era, was equipped with all the modern equipment - electrical system and even wir
radio. In 1917 it was in port in the Philippines when the US Navy siezed the ship fc
in WWI. It was renamed the Sachem. After the war was over, the ship was sold t
Pacific Mail Steamship Company, rechristened the Cuba, and began service betweer
Francisco and Cuba. At that time, it was surveyed and given an A1 rating, the hi
possible. It was traveling down the coast on the very same day, in 1923, when the

troyer tragedy at Honda occurred. That day it ran aground in the very same foul
ther and fog off Point Bennet, on the coast of San Miguel Island. The ship became
)elessly stranded, after trying in vain to get it turned around and back afloat. With
pellors destroyed and listing badly to port, the stricken ship was lost. It slowly broke
rt over the next several months and most of the cargo was successfully salvaged.
'ay, it sits in about 20 feet of water with the wreckage broken up and scattered by the
my seas at:

34° 02.250' N x 120° 27.167' W

This is a treacherous area to navigate with often poor weather, rough seas, substan-
exposed reefs and boiler rocks and strong currents. Nonetheless, the Cuba has some
:llent fishing in better weather with all sorts of shallow water reef fish in abundance
attracting some surface fish action in the milder summer months.

The Cuba is a well known wreck and considerable interest, even today, attracts many
't divers. It is, however, now part of the Channel Islands National Park and marine
eologists have carefully surveyed the site. The following diagram shows the scattered
ains of the famous ship:

The area right around the wreck is calmer than the seas just asea of the site, since
ral natural reefs serve as breakwaters for the wreckage. This means much of the
:kage is in better condition than is to be expected for a ship in such an exposed
tion. The bow, hawsepipes and anchor winch are still very recognizable. Though many
holes have been removed by pillagers, there still remain many of of the fittings,
:s, propellors, boilers, and even sinks and floor tiles from the passenger compart-
ts.

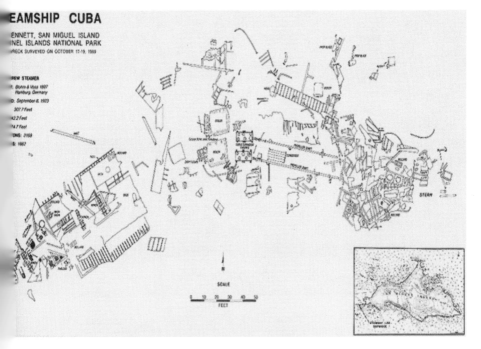

EAMSHIP CUBA

ENNETT, SAN MIGUEL ISLAND
NEL ISLANDS NATIONAL PARK
RECK SURVEYED ON OCTOBER 17-19, 1969

Aggi

The Aggi, a 265 foot long, steel square rigger sailing ship, was launched in 189- Glasgow, Scotland. It was predominantly used for transporting grain around the turr the century. In 1915, with a full load of barley and beans aboard, the ship departed Franciscio being towed by another ship, the Vance. The original plan was for the Vanc tow the Aggi to the Panama Canal where the ship would sail eastward on its own, a crossing into the Atlantic through the canal. Only a short way out of San Francisco, a storm suddenly sprung up, the towline broke, and the Vance left the Aggi on her ow ride out the storm. Because of shifting cargo and other problems, the ship never gai control to navigate on its own. It was tossed about at the whim of the storm until it fir ran aground off Santa Rosa Island. The seawater, streaming in the breached hull, sta saturating the dried grains and, once wet, caused the grain to swell, breaking the ship c from the inside and sending its remains down into the shallow water. It now rests in al 30 feet of water at Talcott Shoals at:

34° 01.000' N x 120° 14.383' W

The Aggi, on the northern end of Santa Rosa Island is better protected than Cuba for fishing but is, nonetheless, in an area reknown for boiler rocks, easily capab poking a hole through the strongest of modern boat hulls. Navigation in this area is for the experienced, but the area has some of the best surface and bass fishing in a

The massive anchor of the Aggi being surveyed by a scientist from the National Parks Services Submerged Resources Center

ifornia. Most years the area of this wreck is festooned with thick stands of kelp pro-
ing the perfect habitat for big Calico Bass, Sheepshead, White Seabass and many other
cies commonly living amongst the kelp forest. In the warmer summer months, Barra-
a, Yellowtail, and Bonito visit the area. In the spring, King Salmon are sometimes
sing through. Bait fishing the rocks and shallow reefs is the most successful tactic with
v trolling swimming plugs a close second. Casting rubber or metal artificial lures is also
ery successful technique both with a quick retrieve for surface feeding species like
racuda and Yellowtail, and also a sinking, twiching retrieve for the ambushing species,
cos, White Seabass, and other reef dwellers.

For the diver, the Aggi is a widely scattered wreck. It is in water of varying depths
n 20 to 65 feet deep. Though much of the wreckage is unrecognizable, looking more
a pile of fish bones than a once proud ship, the fantail stern section is surprisingly
served. The rudder and steering gear lie nearby.

den Horn

The Golden Horn was a bit older than the Aggi, but also built in Scotland in 1883.
ner than steel, its hull was built of iron, heavier and less ductile than the more modern
 hulls. The Golden Horn carried coal. It's last voyage began in New South Wales,
tralia headed for San Pedro with a load of coal. It was passing Santa Rosa Island when
fog moved in and the wind simply quit. The crew could do nothing but wait as the
ng currents drove the drifting ship onto the sharp rocks of the Island. The crew
idoned ship and the heavy swell broke apart the vessel sending it to the bottom. It lies

33° 58.600' N x 120° 13.422 W

Navigation around the Golden Horn is extremely hazardous. Surrounding the wreck
hallow shoals and rocks making it dangerous for boats to anchor over the wreck. It's
r to find a suitable anchorage asea of the wreck then cast toward it. This area is an
llent fishing spot with plenty of reef type fish. Sheepshead, Whitefish, Halfmoons and
h are a staple here. In the winter, White Seabass and Ling Cod patrol these reefs while
e summer months, Barracuda, Bonito and Yellowtail are on the menu. All around the
inel Islands, the fishing is generally good, but where plenty of reefs, natural or in this
an unintended artificial reef, the fishing is truly exceptional.

The Golden Horn is a popular diving spot, Much of the hull remains and in shallow
r. The same cautions about approaching the wreck too closely apply to boats coming
ve the wreck as fish it. The wreckage is still there to see including wire rigging. There
uge section of the center of the hull remaining intact with the keel and frames clearly
e. Bricks from the galley stove are also scattered about the main part of the wreck.
nt archeological surveys have turned up Chinese Abalone fishing camps who used the
en Horn's coal cargo as a convenient fuel when camping on Santa Rosa.

The Golden Horn as it appeared before it met it's fate in 1892

A survey of the Golden Horn being performed by the National Parks service

acock

A ship surrounded in considerable mystery, some say this ship is the Horn-
(AMC-13), but the Hornbill was a commercial fishing boat used by the Navy
minesweeper in WWII and was sunk in the San Francisco area after a colli-
. Others say it is the Spirit of America, but the Navy archives list no such
sel. Still others say it is the Peacock (AM 46), but that ship was a minesweeper
t in 1918 and collided with a Norwegian merchant ship in 1940. Other sources,
the ship as a YMS (Auxiliary Motor Minesweeper) which seems likely since
se ships were of composite construction with steel frames and wooden plank-
which this wreck seems to follow. It's thought the ship sank in the 1970s
out it's engines or propulsion gears. Perhaps it was stripped and scuttled by its
ers or met some other fate. Anyway, it sits in the well protected Scorpion
horage of Santa Cruz Island, so, likely sank while anchored in 65 feet of
er at:

34° 02.955'N x 119 ° 32.868' W

Though not much of a fishing spot, the ship is a great diving site. It sits
ght on a sandy bottom. Although the wood planking is long gone, the hull
es are intact along with tanks and plumbing. There's also substantial debris
n the wreck scattered about on the sandy bottom. Because it sits in a pro-
d cove, this is an easier dive than many of the more exposed wrecks. Much
e allure of this wreck arises from the mystery of why it is there.

*Scorpion Anchorage wreck is most likely a sistership to this YMS, featuring a welded steel frame
but wood planking. The YMS ships were used during WWII for minesweeping.*

Winfield Scott

Back in the gold rush days, the 1850's, California was going through its wild w
period. Plenty of gold was being mined and panned in the Sierra foothills and this bou
ended up being transferred to banks and merchants supplying the goods and services
the newly wealthy miners. The transfer of gold bullion via land routes was a magnet
outlaws looking to get rich quick. Sea routes became the safest method, since attackir
ship at sea was a far more complex task than simply ambushing a stage coach as it roun
a blind bend.

The Winfield Scott, named after the commanding general of the US. Army, a h
of the Mexican American war and presidential candidate, was a steam side wheel s
built in 1850 in New York. It began service between New York and New Orleans
1853, it was purchased by the Pacific Mail Steamship Company and was sailed to
Francisco around the horn, to begin a coastal run between San Francisco and Pana
where its cargo and passengers would be transferred overland to the Atlantic side
Panama, for the sea run to the east coast. This was 50 years before the completion of
Panama Canal.

On the first of December, 1853, the Winfield Scott sailed form San Francisco v
a full load of passengers and gold bullion. The ship was known for its record breal
passages and was far faster than the typical sailing ships of the day. To save some time,
Captain decided to take the Santa Barbara Channel rather than to skirt the outside of
Southern California islands. The visibility worsened and when the ship was turned to
between Santa Cruz and Anacapa Islands, an error in navigation caused the ship to
into a submerged pinnacle of rock just north of Anacapa Island.

At full speed, the wooden hull of the ship was peeled open and it gradually sun
the site. The passengers all left the ship and clamored up on a small rock about 200 y
from the island. The following day, they were ferried, by the ships lifeboats, to the
part of the island. The crew managed to salvage provisions, the mail and much or
passenger's baggage from the rapidly disintegrating ship. It was nearly 10 days before
passengers were rescued from Anacapa by a passing ship.

Major salvage operations were begun in 1894 removing machinery and co
Again, during WWII, when the demand for brass and steel was high, the wreck
"mined" for these metals. More recently, sport divers, lured by much of the unreco
gold, began looting the wreck site. Since becoming a National Park, laws protecting
wreck have begun to be enforced, maintaining the site as a historical site.

The Winfield Scott lies in shallow water, just off the coast of Anacapa Island

34° 00.568' N x 119° 23.247' W

Fishing in the vicinity of the wreck was good, but not really better than anyw
else amongst the shallow reefs of Anacapa. Since the introduction of the Marine Pr
tion Areas, the site is now closed to fishing.

The site is open to sport diving, but remember that it is a crime to disturb or re
any part of the wreck and enforcement of the National Marine Sanctuary regulatic
strict. See the section earlier in this chapter for more information on the NMSs.

Surprisingly, much of the wreck is still present, particularly the machinery. The port ddlewheel's shaft is one of the most prominent pieces, along with boiler bases, huge nze drifts, copper sheathing plates, circular paddlewheel supports, and other partially ognizable pieces. The scatter of the debris remain fairly oriented to their original posi- s in the ship, except that they have been bent around by action of the seas. A survey of scattered remains of the Winfield Scott has been done and the following diagram erated.

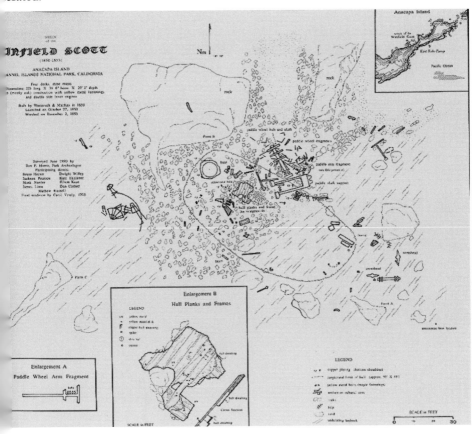

itional Wrecks of the Channel Islands

Following is a chart of the additional wrecks, some well documented, others, yet scovered, in the vicinity of the Channel Islands. They are organized from West to

Channel Islands (San Miguel, Santa Rosa, Santa Cruz & Anacap

Name	Type	Sunk	Reason	Tons	Coordinates	
Galileo		1853	Foundered		34° 05.00' N	122° 45.00
Cuba	Steam screw	1923	Grounded	3168	34° 02.25' N	120° 27.17
Watson A West	Schooner	1923	Stranded	818	34° 02.00' N	120° 27.00
J F West	Schooner	1898	Wrecked		34° 03.00' N	120° 27.00
Anubis		1908			34° 02.00' N	120° 25.00
Comet	Schooner	1911	Stranded	429	34° 03.00' N	120° 23.00
Leader	Schooner	1876			34° 02.07' N	120° 22.03
N B	Otter hunter	1879	Stranded		34° 02.07' N	120° 22.03
J M Coleman	Schooner	1905	Stranded	463	34° 02.07' N	120° 22.03
G W Prescott	Schooner	1879	Wrecked		34° 02.07' N	120° 22.03
Suprise	Schooner	1881	Stranded		34° 02.07' N	120° 22.03
Pectin	Tanker				34° 03.00' N	120° 21.00
Tortuga	LSD	1988	dragged anchor	9375	34° 01.00' N	120° 20.50
Aggi	Bark	1915	tow parted	1898	34° 01.00' N	120° 14.38
Goldenhorn	Bark	1892	Stranded	1842	33° 58.60' N	120° 13.42
Dora Bluhm	Schooner	1910	Stranded	330	33° 57.00' N	120° 12.00
Chickasaw	Steam screw	1962		6131	33° 54.42' N	120° 08.25
Aristocratis		1949			33° 55.00' N	120° 06.00
Blue Fin	Oil screw	1944	Stranded	94	33° 55.00' N	120° 05.00
Crown of England	Steam screw	1894	Grounded	1608	33° 54.82' N	120° 02.92
Brant	Oil screw	1960		149	34° 16.10' N	120° 01.10
Patria	Freighter	1954	Stranded		33° 58.00' N	119° 58.00
Billcoma	Oil screw	1952	Foundered	71	33° 58.00' N	119° 50.00
TBM	Aircraft				33° 57.00' N	119° 49.00
San Buenaventura	Sloop	1858	Sprung seams		34° 00.10' N	119° 45.00
International I	Barge	1918	Stranded	72	34° 00.10' N	119° 45.00
Aurora	Oil screw	1952	Burned	122	34° 00.00' N	119° 45.00
Jane L Stanford	Bark	1929	Collision	970	34° 23.00' N	119° 41.00
Yukon	Schooner	1938	Wrecked		34° 02.00' N	119° 40.00
Black Dolphin					34° 01.00' N	119° 37.00
Thorton		1910	Wrecked		33° 58.00' N	119° 35.00
Golden Gate	Oil screw	1952	Burned	120	33° 59.12' N	119° 33.1
Seaborn		1951			34° 00.00' N	119° 32.00
City of Sausalito	Oil screw	1941	Burned	70	34° 02.00' N	119° 31.0
Nancy Lee		1946			34° 00.00' N	119° 30.0
Bar Bee	Steam screw				34° 00.00' N	119° 25.0
Labor	Gas screw	1924		42	34° 00.00' N	119° 25.0
Coos Bay		1952			34° 00.00' N	119° 24.0
Balboa	Oil screw	1849			34° 00.00' N	119° 24.0
Winfield Scott	Sidewheel Steam	1853	Grounded	1291	34° 00.57' N	119° 23.2
Del Rio	Oil screw	1952	Burned	110	34° 00.00' N	119° 23.0
Gypsy Q		1955	Wrecked		34° 01.00' N	119° 23.0
Equator	Oil screw	1949		238	34° 00.33' N	119° 22.8
San Guiseppe	Oil screw	1950	Burned	109	33° 56.00' N	119° 22.0
TBM	Aircraft				34° 01.00' N	119° 22.0
San Francisco	Oil screw	1949	Burned	128	34° 01.00' N	119° 19.5
Saint Anne	Oil screw	1955	Foundered	100	33° 46.05' N	118° 40.1

Chapter 5
Northern Los Angeles County

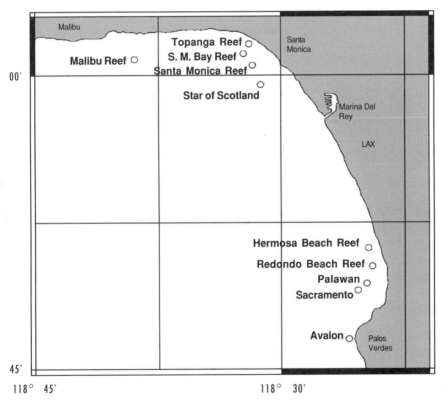

The Northern part of LA county, for purposes of this book, includes the coastline
[Ma]libu south to Palos Verdes including Santa Monica Bay, the coast around Los
[Ange]les airport and the south bay areas of Manhattan, Hermosa and Redondo Beach to
[Kin]gy Point, the start of the Palos Verdes peninsula. There are a large number of both
[inten]tional artificial reefs, built as fish attractants by the California Department of Fish and
[Gam]e, and unintentional artificial reefs, shipwrecks, that operate just as effectively as at-
[tracta]nts of fish. The two major small craft ports in the area are Marina Del Rey and King
[Harb]or in Redondo Beach. Both of these ports have easy access to the many reefs and
[wrec]ks in the area.

Malibu Artificial Reef

The Malibu Artificial Reef was one of the original artificial reefs built by the Califo-nia Department of Fish and Game. It was built in 1961 of 14 automobile bodies, o streetcar, 44 concrete shelters, and 333 tons of quarry rock. The car bodies and street have long since disappeared from the ravages of seawater. It covers an area of about acre and lies in 60 feet of water off the coast of Malibu. The relief is about two feet the sandy, silty bottom. There are two distinct rock piles distinguishable now. They're

A - 34° 0.800' N x 118° 38.983' W
B - 34° 0.817' N x 118° 39.083' W

The Malibu artificial reef has plenty of smaller perch, good Sculpin fishing in early spring, and Halibut and Sand Bass along the bottom in the vicinity.

Topanga Artificial Reef

This reef was built in 1987 of 10,000 tons of quarry rock in about 28 foot d water off the Topanga Beach. It has about a 3 foot relief off the sandy bottom. The is about 13 acres in three distinct areas:

A - 34° 01.550' N x 118° 31.817' W
B - 34° 01.600' N x 118° 31.933' W
C - 34° 01.767' N x 118° 32.067' W

This reef grows a substantial canopy of kelp when the water is cooler. It was o

Scrap and surplus concrete pipes are a popular and effective artificial reef material.

ly intended to be a bass habitat and has succeeded well. Plenty of Calicos inhabit the
f as well as Sand Bass around the edges. Don't forget to check for Halibut in the sandy
tom surrounding the reef.

nta Monica Bay Artificial Reef

This huge complex of rock piles was built in 1987 for the express purpose of
ancing the fishing and has been a rousing success. There are 24 separate rock piles
de up of 20,000 tons of quarry rock covering an area of something like 256 acres. The
S targets are as follows:

1. 34° 00.767 N x 118° 31.900 W
2. 34° 00.850 N x 118° 32.050 W
3. 34° 01.035 N x 118° 32.163 W
4. 34° 01.097 N x 118° 32.295 W
5. 34° 01.177 N x 118° 32.427 W
6. 34° 01.323 N x 118° 32.683 W
7. 34° 01.377 N x 118° 32.815 W
8. 34° 01.267 N x 118° 32.867 W
9. 34° 00.483 N x 118° 32.067 W
10. 34° 00.602 N x 118° 32.037 W
11. 34° 00.692 N x 118° 32.167 W
12. 34° 00.705 N x 118° 32.300 W
13. 34° 00.785 N x 118° 32.438 W
14. 34° 00.842 N x 118° 32.427 W
15. 34° 00.833 N x 118° 32.900 W
16. 34° 00.950 N x 118° 33.050 W
17. 34° 00.150 N x 118° 32.233 W
18. 34° 00.297 N x 118° 32.222 W
19. 34° 00.283 N x 118° 32.433 W
20. 34° 00.350 N x 118° 32.617 W
21. 34° 00.450 N x 118° 32.800 W
22. 34° 00.533 N x 118° 32.983 W
23. 34° 00.633 N x 118° 33.083 W
24. 34° 00.650 N x 118° 33.250 W

The Santa Monica Bay reef has been known as probably the premier Halibut fishing
e in Southern California. In addition, it gets its share of Sand Bass, Sculpin, and many
r species.

a Monica Artificial Reef

This is another of the original 1961 reefs like the Malibu reef. It started with 4 car
es, 1 streetcar, 330 tons of quarry rock and 44 concrete shelters. In 1971 it was added
th the addition of 100 tons of concrete pier pilings. It covers a ½ acre site in 3 distinct
over the mostly sandy and silty bottom rising to a relief of nearly 4 feet. The coor-
es are:

A. 34° 00.567 N x 118° 31.820 W
B. 34° 00.550 N x 118° 31.800 W
C. 34° 00.550 N x 118° 31.840 W

The reef isn't nearly as productive for the fisherman as the Santa Monica Bay r(
but has it's good days of Sand bass and Sculpin fishing.

Star of Scotland

The Star of Scotland was originally commissioned in 1918 as the HMS Mistlet
The ship was originally used as a decoy destroyer of World War I German submarir
Unlike in WWII, when the torpedo reigned as the supreme submarine weapon, in W'
often submarines would approach merchant vessels submerged, then when close enou
surface and attack the ship with their deck guns. Well, the Star had a nasty surprise wai(
for the hapless u-boat. When the sub surfaced, steel panels would drop, exposing guns
the faux merchantman's deck, blazing rapid fire back at the submarine, used to leisu:
picking off defenseless prey.

The Star of Scotland went through many names from it's WWI beginnings as
Royal Navy's Mistletoe. It was named the Chiapas, carrying cargo between San Franci
and Panama. Later it became the La Playa de Ensenada and was used to haul fruit fr
Mexico to California. After reaching Santa Monica Bay, it became a speakeasy and g:
bling ship during prohibition, where it went through another four name changes. It is :

said to have bee
floating bordellc
1940 it was ch
tened the Star
Scotland, its f
name, where
served as a p:
boat and fish
barge.

In Janu
1942, a series
storms pumm(
the coast of Cal:
nia. The Star
Scotland started
ing on water tha
bilge pu:
couldn't han

Most shipwrecks will grow substantial marine life, like these anemones

Those aboard reported that something had given way, and the ship started sinking qui
from a huge inrush of seawater. One crewman was killed, but the rest were rescue
now sits about 2 miles off the coast of Santa Monica in about 60 feet of water at:

33° 59.520' N x 118° 31.274' W

The Star of Scotland is an excellent fish attractant. Divers say there are plenty of
ıck Seabass inhabiting the wreck. These giants are protected in California, and to take
e is punishable by stiff fines, so, if you hook one, please return it to the depths un-
rmed. Other reef species like Calico Bass, Halfmoons and Perch are abundant in and
ound the wreck. Also, flats species like Halibut, Sandbass and Sculpin are plentiful here.

Diving the wreck is popular among sport divers, and its near complete condition
.kes it a fascinating underwater treasure. It has been down there for 60 years now and
:iodically, sections of the structure collapse, so it is dangerous to enter any part of the
eck, and strongly discouraged even by experienced wreck divers. Many days this area
; poor visibility, but on the occasional good visibility days, the Star is a spectacular sight,
:rusted with purple anemones and rock scallops.

:rmosa Beach Artificial Reef

One of the earliest artificial reefs in Southern California, the Hermosa Beach artificial
·f lies in 60 feet of water only about a mile North of the King Harbor channel entrance.
vas built in 1960 of 14 car bodies, 1 streetcar, 330 tons of quarry rock and 44 concrete
.lters. Of course, the sea swallowed up the car bodies and streetcar long ago, but the
k and concrete shelters remain in a scattered field covering about ½ acre. The center of
field is located:

33° 51.217' N x 118° 24.783' W

The relief of the reef is very low, more like cobble beds, and it attracts some Bass,
:h and other smaller fish species. The sandy area adjacent to the reefs is good Halibut
Sand Bass habitat and in the spring, the Sculpin abound here.

londo Beach Artificial Reef

A very large and complex reef, the Redondo Beach Artificial reef was started in
2 with 1000 tons of quarry rock. It was added to in 1974 with the addition of a barge,
975 with 350 tons of cement pipe, in 1976 with 700 tons of concrete pilings, in 1976
ı 700 tons of concrete pilings and in 1979 with 1500 concrete floats. It now encom-
.es over 1.6 acres. The main targets in the reef are located at:

A. 33° 50.300' N x 118° 24.567' W
B. 33° 50.300' N x 118° 24.550' W
C. 33° 50.283' N x 118° 24.517' W
D. 33° 50.267' N x 118° 24.550' W
E. 33° 50.250' N x 118° 24.517' W
F. 33° 50.233' N x 118° 24.567' W
G. 33° 50.233' N x 118° 24.533' W
H. 33° 50.234' N x 118° 24.500' W
I. 33° 50.217' N x 118° 24.550' W
J. 33° 50.200' N x 118° 24.567' W
K. 33° 50.183' N x 118° 24.517' W

This is one of the finer reefs to fish in the area. It holds excellent numbers of a wi variety of fish. In addition to Bass and Perch, Sheepshead, Whitefish and Sculpin, otl reef dwellers are available as well. In the warmer months, pelagic species like Barracu Bonito and even Yellowtail can be seen cruising the surface chasing the schools of t circling the area looking for shelter from predators.

Palawan

The Palawan was built in 1944 as part of the huge numbers of cargo vessels built carry materials of war and supplies to our troops and allies overseas. These "liberty shi were based on an older British design and were mass produced in an amazing technic pioneered by the famous industrialist Henry Kaiser, who, surprisingly, had never buil ship. They were a huge success and were a major player in the allied victory in WWII. T 441 foot long ship was scuttled in 110 feet of water in 1977. The next year, 1978, 6(cubic yards of rubble were added to the site. It lies at:

33° 49.417 N x 118° 24.883 W

The Palawan has great fishing. For a while, a fishing barge was anchored over wreck but the barge is long gone. All reef species including bigger Ling Cod, inhabit wreck. Plenty of Halibut, Sand Bass, and Sculpin surround it, and in the warmer mon surface feeding pelagic species patrol all around the big ship

Diving the Palawan is quite an experience because of the ship's sheer size. The was stripped before scuttling, and the superstructure and machinery removed. The w is 125 feet deep at the base of the empty hull. Since it was scuttled to create a fish attrac and artificial reef, there is a considerable amount of lost fishing tackle attached to collapsing structure.

The Palawan liberty ship underway as she appeared during World War II

cramento

The Sacramento was built in 1877 to be used as a San Francisco Bay ferry shuttling
ssengers and cars between Oakland and San Francisco. It was a steam powered
ewheeler. It was completely rebuilt in 1923 and continued to work until 1954. The
mpletion of the San Francisco Bay bridge doomed the regular ferry service across the
. It was towed to Southern California and converted to a fishing barge anchored off
 coast of Redondo Beach. Fishermen would get shuttled back and forth all day by a
i boat to fish from the decks of the ferry. In the winter it was towed back into King
rbor to ride out the winter storms. When the summer arrived, it was towed back into
sition for the fishing season. In a storm in December 1968, the barge took on too
ch water and sunk into 180 feet of water. Ironically, the next fishing barge was an-
ored right over the old wreck where it served as an artificial reef. It lies:

33° 49.017 N x 118° 25.367 W

Like the Palawan, the Sacramento is a great place to fish. Since it lies in deeper water,
ets many exotic reef species. It's perched on the edge of Redondo Canyon so during
 winter time, squid spawns attract Ling Cod, White Sea Bass, Sable fish and other
cies not commonly found in shallower reefs.

The wreck of the Sacramento is in fairly good shape, offering the diver a chance to
 the famous ship submerged. Original stained glass windows, wood carvings and brass
ngs remain as they were during the ferry boat's heyday. After it sunk, the Sacramento
 used as an artificial reef for yet another fishing barge anchored over the wreck, so
y fishing lines and weights now festoon the ship.

The Sacramento doing its ferry duty before conversion to a fishing barge

lon

The Avalon was a steam powered passenger ship, 269 feet long, built in 1891 in
eland Ohio, and named the S. S. Virginia. Her first job was to shuttle passengers
een Chicago and Milwaukee on Lake Michigan. The Navy took over the ship in 1918

for the needs of WWI and renamed the ship U.S.S. Blueridge, and sailed it to Bost
After the war ended, the Navy sold the ship as scrap to William Wrigley, the owner
Catalina Island and the man who's chewing gum made his name famous. He had the sh
moved to the west coast and renamed it the Avalon after Catalina's main harbor. The sh
was used between Avalon and the Port of Los Angeles until WWII when the Navy ag
needed the ship for wartime purposes. After the war it was returned to Wrigley. In 196
was sold for scrap and converted to a salvage barge for the wreck of the ship "Domi
tor" that had run aground at Point Vicente and is visible yet today along the Palos Ver
shoreline. While at anchor in 1964, a storm broke the ship loose and turned it broadside
the waves. After hours of pownding the ship swamped and sank in about 70 feet
water at:

33° 46.567 N x 118° 25.917 W

The Avalon is usually a very good surface fishing spot, with Calico Bass, Barracu
and Bonito in the warmer months and sometimes Yellowtail. The bottom features m
reef species as well, including Whitefish, Sheepshead, and Perch.

Diving the Avalon is a bit underwhelming these days, Since the ship lies along
exposed side of the Palos Verdes penninsula, the degrading effects of the sea and wea
have reduced the wreckage to some barely recognizable beams along the bottom. It is
a rocky bottom, so cannot bury itself like some other wrecks lying on soft bottoms,
kelp, and other marine plant growth renders the remaining structure barely recognizabl
once having been a ship.

The Avalon as it appeared in 1924

Propellor shafts, like this beauty are the most likely parts of ships to survive the ravages of time and the ocean.

...litional Wrecks in Northern Los Angeles County

Following is the database for wrecks in this area. They're arranged from North to ...th by wreck location:

Northern Los Angeles County

Name	Type	Sunk	Reason	Tons	Coordinates	
Minnie A Caine	fishing bge	1939	Parted anchor		34° 02.17' N	118° 33.33'
Ameco		1930	Swamped		34° 02.10' N	118° 34.13'
Amie	Bark	1882	Grounded	628	34° 02.00' N	119° 31.03'
American Boy	Oil screw	1956		130	34° 01.50' N	118° 41.00'
Astorian		1937			34° 00.08' N	118° 48.33'
Horizon	Oil screw	1932	Burned	69	34° 00.00' N	118° 48.00'
George E Billings	Schooner	1941	Wrecked	1260	34° 00.00' N	118° 29.25'
Defender		1940			34° 00.00' N	118° 48.00'
Aristozehis		1954			34° 00.00' N	118° 30.00'
L Padre		1956			34° 00.00' N	118° 48.00'
Western Fisher		1948	Wrecked		34° 00.00' N	118° 48.00'
W T Co #3	Barge	1935	Foundered	264	34° 00.00' N	119° 10.00
Oriental	Oil screw`	1930	Stranded	66	34° 00.00' N	118° 48.00
Star of Hollywood	fishing barge	1942			33° 59.08' N	118° 31.20
Star of Scotland	Steam screw	1942	sprung seams	1250	33° 59.08' N	118° 31.20
Los Angeles TC #1 Barge		1921	Foundered	52	33° 59.00' N	118° 29.00
Sea Products #2	Barge	1917	Stranded	75	33° 59.00' N	118° 30.00
Bacchus	Barge	1926	Wrecked	311	33° 59.00' N	118° 29.00
Tennessee		1942			33° 58.00' N	118° 32.00
Sea Products #4	Barge	1917	Stranded	111	33° 57.00' N	118° 28.00
Falcon		1945			33° 55.30' N	118° 25.92
Crowley #64		1949	Foundered	267	33° 55.00' N	118° 30.00
Pilgram		1852	Burned		33° 55.00' N	118° 50.00
Putnik	Gas screw	1926		35	33° 55.00' N	118° 57.00
J D Rice	Brig	1867	Stranded		33° 53.00' N	118° 24.67
Sea King	Oil screw	1956		132	33° 51.00' N	118° 32.00
Katie Flickinger	Barkentine	1905	Stranded	472	33° 50.00' N	118° 23.50
D C Murray		1889			33° 50.00' N	118° 23.50
Georgina	Bark	1935	Stranded	998	33° 50.00' N	118° 23.50
Irene	Barge	1937		772	33° 50.00' N	118° 23.50
Fullerton	Barkentine	1927		1554	33° 50.00' N	118° 23.50
Gardiner City	Bark	1904	Stranded		33° 50.00' N	118° 23.50
Pan Pacific	Oil screw	1950	Foundered	226	33° 50.00' N	118° 55.0
Columbia #41		1941	Foundered	483	33° 50.00' N	118° 28.0
Annie Gee	Schooner	1897		147	33° 50.00' N	118° 23.5
C D Murray		1888			33° 50.00' N	118° 23.5
Novus		1940			33° 50.00' N	118° 23.5
National City		1907			33° 50.00' N	118° 23.5
William Bowden	Schooner	1926	Stranded	778	33° 50.00' N	118° 23.5
Mabel Gray	Schooner	1904	Wrecked	205	33° 50.00' N	118° 23.5
Spare Time	Fishing boat	1952	Explosion		33° 50.00' N	118° 38.0
Thomas P Emigh		1932	Stranded	1040	33° 49.83' N	118° 23.9
Retriever	Barge	1951	Foundered	99	33° 49.42' N	118° 24.8
Palawan	Liberty Shp	1977	sunk for reef	14250	33° 49.42' N	118° 24.8
Sacramento	Ferry	1968		87	33° 49.02' N	118° 25.3
Georgina	Barge	1966		96	33° 49.00' N	118° 25.0
Unknown	Jetliner				33° 48.00' N	118° 30.0
Gratia	Steel Bark	1933	Wrecked	1582	33° 48.00' N	118° 24.6
Unknown	Junk				33° 47.33' N	118° 25.0
Arkansas		1941			33° 46.75' N	119° 10.3
Avalon	Steam screw	1960	parted anchor	1985	33° 46.57' N	118° 25.9
Eagle	Gas screw	1937	Burned	77	33° 46.53' N	118° 12.3
Garcia					33° 46.42' N	118° 25.6
Dominator	Liberty ship	1960	stranded	7176	33° 46.40' N	118° 25.4
Washtenaw	Steam screw	1928	Abandoned	2896	33° 46.00' N	118° 15.0
Golden State	Schooner	1937		570	33° 46.00' N	118° 14.0
Unknown	Tug				33° 46.00' N	118° 14.0
Unknown	Schooner				33° 46.00' N	118° 14.0
Cricket	Sidewheel	1885		60	33° 46.00' N	118° 15.0

Northern Los Angeles County (cont.)

Name	Type	Sunk	Reason	Tons	Coordinates	
C Co #6	Barge	1943	Stranded	490	33° 45.83' N	118° 11.00' W
proco #2	Barge	1917	Stranded	91	33° 45.83' N	118° 11.00' W
orm King		1956			33° 45.50' N	118° 16.25' W
C #1	Barge	1958		62	33° 45.50' N	118° 16.00' W
ver Strand	Ferry	1970			33° 45.50' N	118° 16.25' W
rkay	Tanker	1947	Explosion	10342	33° 45.27' N	118° 16.08' W
	Schooner	1935		142	33° 45.00' N	118° 13.00' W
known	Barge				33° 45.00' N	118° 15.00' W
n H Marion		1946			33° 45.00' N	118° 11.00' W
ate Galleon	Ship	1930			33° 45.00' N	118° 10.00' W
known	Hull remains				33° 45.00' N	118° 15.00' W
egon Trader	Barge	1949			33° 45.00' N	118° 11.00' W
nterey	Barkentine	1935		1854	33° 45.00' N	118° 14.00' W
nes F McKenna	Scow	1960			33° 45.00' N	118° 11.00' W

When diving wrecks in reduced visibility, coming upon the wreck is like seeing a ghostly image arising out of the mist

41

Chapter 6
Southern Los Angeles County

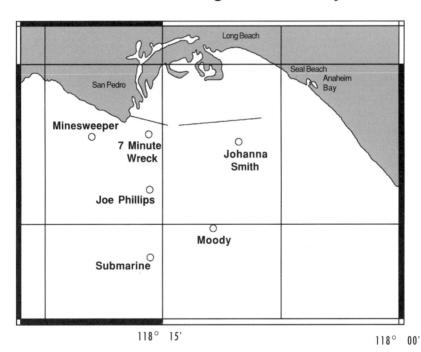

Though there are no Department of Fish and Game created artificial reefs in the [...] of Los Angeles area, there are a substantial number of shipwrecks in there, in shallow [...] gh water, to make for interesting fishing spots.

[...]esweeper

The minesweeper fishing spot has been a commonly visited wreck in the area. There's [...] ately a wreck there, but it doesn't seem to correspond to any of the known wreck [...] ase coordinates. It's located:

33° 41.605 N x 118° 19.455 W

The minesweeper is predominantly a surface fishing area and is known for its abi[
to attract springtime Barracuda runs. Don't discount it for Yellowtail, though. It's too d
for sport diving.

7 Minute Wreck

One of the most famous wrecks out of Los Angeles harbor, the 7 minute Wrec[
the F. S. Loop, a steam powered lumber schooner about 193 feet long. It was being tov
out of the harbor when it sank. Since it came to rest in fairly shallow water, and to m
sure it wasn't a hazard to other ships, the Coast Guard decided to blow it up. Over a
of TNT was packed into the ship and - - - kaboom! - no more hazard. The 7 min
wreck is only 1 mile from the Angel's Gate entrance to LA Harbor at:

33° 41.743' N x 118° 15.912' W

The shipweck is fairly low relief, only ribs sticking out of the bottom and scatte
wreckage, so it isn't exactly a fish haven, but it does attract its share of Perch, Blacksn
and occasionally Calicos and Sand Bass. The surrounding muddy bottom has Halibut.

Similarly, the wreck also isn't much of a dive site . There is scattered wreckage,
the visibility in this area, due to extensive ship traffic, is generally poor to miserable.
scattered wreckage these days is barely recognizable as manmade.

Johanna Smith

The Johanna Smith was one of the famous gambling ships operating out of the
Angeles area in the roaring 20s. A mysterious fire destroyed the ship in 1932. It didn't
from the fire though, only rolled over and stayed afloat at anchor. The Coast G[
placed explosive charges on the ship and eventually got it to the bottom and out o[
way of passing ships. The wreckage is only scattered debris now. It sits in 80 feet of v

The Johanna Smith in her heyday as a gambling ship

33° 41.388' N x 118° 10.144' W

The Johanna Smith is a good attractant of bait, so often will save an otherwise [su]nked day. In the spring, the Barracuda frequently circle the wreck chasing bait and all [ove]r, the Bass seem to find life here pretty good. The flats around the wreck often have [san]d Bass, Sculpin and Halibut also.

Because the hull was destroyed by explosion, and the action of the sea, this wreck [has] been has been reduced to three small piles of machinery and debris sitting on the [bot]tom. It is fairly close to Los Angeles harbor so the visibility is often poor due to the [bo]at traffic and general industrial activity. For these reasons, it is rarely visited by divers. For [tho]se who venture here, the wreck is usually overgrown with sea life so is indistinguishable [fro]m a natural rock outcropping.

Phillips

The Joe Phillips was a rock barge that sank in a storm while transporting quarry [roc]k. There is very little published about the wreck since it's in water too deep for divers [to s]how much interest in. It's in 175 feet of water at:

33° 39.082' N x 118° 16.076' W

The Joe Phillips is pretty much a deep reef, Rock Cod fishing proposition, though it [doe]s get its share of bigger Lings during the winter months. The sandy bottom around [the] wreck is also a good Sand Dab area all year round. I've also heard of a few bigger [Hali]but surrounding the wreck for those who like fishing for these species in deeper water. [Som]etimes big trophys come up from the deep.

[Mo]ody

The USS Moody was a WWI era destroyer, built in 1918. It served the Navy well [thro]ughout the 1920s as a first line fighting ship and served throughout the Pacific. In [1931], though with the depression and cutbacks in defense spending, the ship was decom[miss]ioned and sent to the scrap yard at Mare Island. MGM studios had a movie in the [work]s called "Hell Below," when they spotted the ship, thinking its shape was close enough [to a] German WWI warship, so they bought the Moody for the movie. They packed [dyna]mite in the ship to simulate a torpedo hit and in February 1933, with cameras rolling, [they] blew the ship in a spectacular detonation that sent the ship to the bottom of the [shall]ow water off Los Angeles harbor. It lies in two pieces in 140 feet of water at:

33° 37.417' N x 118° 12.130' W
33° 37.446' N x 118° 12.150' W

Many fishermen know this wreck simply as "the destroyer." It's known as a good [fishin]g spot attracting plenty of Bass, both Calicos in the wreck and Sand Bass around it. [Lin]g, Sculpin, Sheepshead, and Whitefish abound here also. Occasionally White Seabass visit the wreck, as do Ling Cod in the late winter and early spring.

The Moody laid in its watery grave from 1933 until 1973 when sport divers fou the two halves of the ship. They lie over 100 feet apart in 140 feet of water. The st section is sitting upright with its bronze propellers still in-place. The bow section is on side, on the sandy bottom. The visibility is generally pretty good, but since the wreck is deep, a good light is needed. The wreck is fairly complete, except for the demolished section, with most of its brass fittings still present. Sudden strong currents in this area make a dive of this depth dangerous and several incautious divers have lost their li here.

The USS Moody, DD-277 as it appeared in the early 1920s after its WWI duty and before its sacrifice to the movie industry

Submarine

Deck hands on party boats will all swear this fishing spot is a Japanese subma sunk by the Fort MacArthur guns, atop the Palos Verdes peninsula during WWII. This urban legend. No such event ever occurred - at least not by any accounts I've ever c across. It is possible this is the submarine UB-88, sunk for US Navy gunnery practi 1921. But the coordinates don't match up so well, and photos of the recently re-dis ered UB-88 seem to suggest the real UB-88 lies in shallower water. Nonetheless, this great secret spot fishing hole. It's at:

33° 35.901' N x 118° 15.838' W

The Submarine is in about 240 feet of water, so has deeper water fish. The ope story of this book, when I describe landing a big Ling Cod is a true story and took fishing this spot. Expect Red Rockfish mostly here, including Reds, Boccacio, Starry. Chilipeppers during most of the year and add Ling Cod to the mix if fishing in late w or early spring. You also might haul up a Black Sea Bass, White Sea Bass or other e here since there seems to be plenty of cover and caves down there for bigger fish. sandy bottom surrounding the wreck is carpeted with Sand Dabs and the occas Halibut. As this book is being published, it is illegal to fish for some of these sp so keep current on the DF&G regulations.

Calico Bass, like this fat beauty are a staple game fish around wrecks and reefs.

...itional Wrecks in Southern Los Angeles County

Following is the database for wrecks in this area. They're arranged from North to ...th by wreck location:

Name	Type	Sunk	Reason	Tons	Coordinates	
Southern Los Angeles County						
Hancock	Steam screw	1863	Explosion	83	33° 44.50' N	118° 16.25' W
ic Prince		1928			33° 44.50' N	118° 16.25' W
aweli	Barkentine	1935	Stranded	899	33° 44.50' N	118° 25.00' W
ppine	Schooner	1934	Stranded	523	33° 44.50' N	118° 16.33' W
eral Lane	Schooner	1855			33° 44.50' N	118° 16.25' W
t Coast Summer		1948			33° 44.50' N	118° 16.25' W
	Oil yawl	1933	Grounded	124	33° 44.42' N	118° 24.67' W
berry		1894			33° 44.42' N	118° 24.67' W
patra		1941			33° 44.42' N	118° 24.67' W
a	Barkentine	1933	Stranded	1067	33° 44.42' N	118° 24.67' W
pern	Steam screw	1895	Grounded	943	33° 44.42' N	118° 24.67' W
er		1947	Wrecked		33° 44.42' N	118° 24.67' W
r Gate		1948			33° 44.40' N	118° 24.73' W
C #9	Barge	1940	Foundered	161	33° 44.33' N	118° 25.00' W
ican Girl	Oil screw	1951			33° 44.17' N	118° 22.00' W
e	Oil screw	1932			33° 44.00' N	118° 16.00' W
on					33° 44.00' N	118° 16.00' W
ow	Gas yawl	1926	Burned	91	33° 44.00' N	118° 10.00' W
co #3	Barge	1921	Stranded	99	33° 44.00' N	118° 15.00' W
e M Phelps	Bark	1896		2998	33° 44.00' N	118° 16.00' W
ta		1952			33° 44.00' N	118° 16.00' W
own	Cabin cruiser				33° 44.00' N	118° 14.00' W
own					33° 44.00' N	118° 08.00' W
	Power sch.	1930		1425	33° 44.00' N	118° 15.50' W

Southern Los Angeles County (cont.)

Name	Type	Sunk	Reason	Tons	Coordinates	
Anaconda		1946			33° 44.00' N	118° 26.00
Mary Jane	Schooner	1849	Stranded		33° 43.80' N	118° 16.67
C C Co. #26	Barge	1961		111	33° 43.75' N	118° 06.00
Pierpoint Queen		1951			33° 43.62' N	118° 11.70
La Sota	Gas yawl	1915	Burned	55	33° 43.50' N	118° 16.25
Kennebec		1887	Storm	2000	33° 43.50' N	118° 16.25
Liberty Girl	Oil screw	1942	Stranded	57	33° 43.50' N	118° 16.25
Jorie		1943			33° 43.50' N	118° 16.25
Koloa	Brig	1876			33° 43.50' N	118° 16.25
Danube	Brigantine	1828	Stranded		33° 43.50' N	118° 16.25
Esperia #3	Oil screw	1952	Foundered	110	33° 43.42' N	118° 10.00
Melrose	Ferry	1932	dragged anchor	2662	33° 43.08' N	118° 19.42
Irene	Schooner	1929	Burned	722	33° 43.00' N	118° 10.00
Respigadera		1888	Grounded	2583	33° 43.00' N	118° 16.50
LSC 127	Landing Cft	1945	Wrecked		33° 43.00' N	118° 16.8
Gleaner		1906			33° 43.00' N	118° 16.00
Unknown	Bait barge				33° 43.00' N	118° 10.0
LCT 1358	Landing Cft	1945	Wrecked		33° 43.00' N	118° 16.8
Sierra	Steam screw	1926		1286	33° 42.75' N	118° 14.5
Gipsy Girl	Oil screw	1945		56	33° 42.50' N	118° 15.0
Explorer		1929	Grounded		33° 42.33' N	118° 15.5
Adelaide Cooper	Bark	1879	Stranded	297	33° 42.33' N	118° 15.5
H M Storey	Steam screw				33° 42.28' N	118° 17.6
Mississippi		1924			33° 42.28' N	118° 17.6
Aquila		1949			33° 42.28' N	118° 17.6
Hwa Tung		1946			33° 42.28' N	118° 17.6
Saint Louis	Bark	1887	Grounded	276	33° 42.28' N	118° 17.6
Unknown	Sailboat				33° 42.28' N	118° 17.6
Rocona	Oil screw	1963			33° 42.28' N	118° 17.6
Robert Mills		1946			33° 42.25' N	118° 17.6
David C Meyer	Steam screw	1926	Stranded	2510	33° 42.17' N	118° 17.5
Southern Explorer	Oil screw	1968		130	33° 42.00' N	118° 17.0
Avalon	Gas screw	1926			33° 42.00' N	118° 18.0
Annie M Rolph	Bark	1942	Wrecked	1393	33° 42.00' N	118° 10.0
San Ubaldo		1926			33° 42.00' N	118° 20.0
Johanna Smith	Steam screw	1932	Burned	1844	33° 42.00' N	118° 11.5
Melrose	Schooner	1938		615	33° 42.00' N	118° 17.0
Gosling		1958			33° 42.00' N	118° 16.0
Naughty Queen	Oil screw	1974		278	33° 42.00' N	118° 14.0
Little Butte		1946			33° 42.00' N	118° 15.0
Saint Joseph	Oil screw	1975		60	33° 42.00' N	118° 19.0
Casino	Bark	1935	explosion & fire	1274	33° 42.00' N	118° 08.5
City of Florence		1900			33° 41.50' N	118° 17.0
Bahada	Steam tug	1923		132	33° 41.25' N	118° 15.0
Nelson		1936			33° 41.00' N	118° 17.0
Benita		1951			33° 41.00' N	118° 18.0
Unknown	Wreckage				33° 41.00' N	118° 13.0
Unknown	Fishing boat				33° 41.00' N	118° 19.0
Georgia Straits	Tug				33° 40.00' N	118° 12.0
El Padre	Oil screw	1951			33° 40.00' N	118° 10.0
Saint James	Oil screw	1949	Burned	149	33° 39.40' N	118° 21.0
Olympic #2	Barge	1940	Collision	1766	33° 39.07' N	118° 13.0
Moody	Destroyer	1933	sunk for movie	1308	33° 38.00' N	118° 09.0
UB-88	Submarine	1921	gunfire	640	33° 38.00' N	118° 09.0
Discovery	Oil screw	1955	Burned	123	33° 30.00' N	118° 10.0

Chapter 7
Orange County

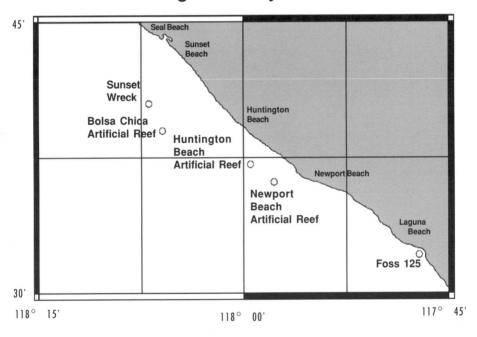

The Orange County coastal waters have their share of both manmade fish attracting and also sunken ships serving as fish havens.

...et Wreck

I've been unable to determine exactly which sunken ship this is but it's fairly close to ...e an old 286 ton schooner, built in 1881, called the Lottie Carson sank many years ...The relief is low, barely recognizable on a bottom meter but something is sure out ...e. It's located:

33° 40.491' N x 118° 06.977' W

The Sunset wreck is primarily a surface fishing spot with schools of Barracuda of visiting the area in search of bait fish. In addition, the bottom has Barred Sand Bass a Sculpin on occasion. It's not a great spot, but sometimes the action can be good.

Low relief, very deteriorated wreckage and poor visibility make this wreck no particularly interesting or desirable dive site. Lots of ship traffic is in the area and so times ships anchor right over the spot.

Bolsa Chica Artificial Reef

The huge Bolsa Chica artificial reef complex is a major construction accompl ment. It covers nearly 220 acres off the coast of the Bolsa Chica wetlands prese nestled beween Huntington Beach and Sunset Beach (Huntington Harbor.) There are separate rock piles organized in somewhat of a double row. It was built with 12,000 t of concrete rubble and 8 steel and concrete barges, beginning in 1988. It is continu being added to and the Department of Fish and Game has plans to add even more to complex. It lies several miles offshore in 85 to 100 feet of water in the muddy bottom the Huntington Flats area. The targets from North to South are:

1. 33° 39.548' N x 118° 06.048' W
2. 33° 39.540' N x 118° 05.925' W
3. 33° 39.495' N x 118° 05.803' W
4. 33° 39.487' N x 118° 05.952' W
5. 33° 39.447' N x 118° 05.820' W
6. 33° 39.437' N x 118° 05.967' W
7. 33° 39.403' N x 118° 05.843' W
8. 33° 39.350' N x 118° 06.133' W
9. 33° 39.327' N x 118° 06.062' W
10. 33° 39.300' N x 118° 06.183' W
11. 33° 39.287' N x 118° 06.128' W
12. 33° 39.262' N x 118° 05.968' W
13. 33° 39.250' N x 118° 05.833' W
14. 33° 39.250' N x 118° 06.200' W
15. 33° 39.217' N x 118° 06.073' W
16. 33° 39.216' N x 118° 06.166' W
17. 33° 39.172' N x 118° 05.992' W
18. 33° 39.111' N x 118° 05.913' W
19. 33° 39.068' N x 118° 05.934' W
20. 33° 39.033' N x 118° 05.948' W
21. 33° 39.020' N x 118° 06.168' W
22. 33° 38.987' N x 118° 05.958' W
23. 33° 38.978' N x 118° 06.105' W
24. 33° 38.967' N x 118° 06.292' W
25. 33° 38.945' N x 118° 05.978' W
26. 33° 38.906' N x 118° 05.993' W
27. 33° 38.867' N x 118° 06.018' W
28. 33° 38.817' N x 118° 06.343' W

29. 33° 38.815' N x 118° 06.025' W
30. 33° 38.773' N x 118° 06.048' W
31. 33° 38.713' N x 118° 06.106' W
32. 33° 38.317' N x 118° 05.940' W

The Bolsa Chica artificial reef is a bass fisherman's dream. Calico Bass and Sand
s abound here and respond to just about any standard bass fishing technique. They're
 all year round, but in the late spring, throughout the summer and into early fall, the
ng is at its prime. In addition to bass, there are plenty of Sculpin, awaiting a piece of
squid to come drifting by, as well as a host of other Perch, Croakers, Whitefish,
pshead and other species. In the spring and summer, the Barracuda can be found
ing the structure picking off smaller reef dwellers. There have also been quite a few
 Yellowtail landed from this reef in the past few years. In all, this is a must GPS
oint to store for anyone wanting to productively fish the area.

tington Beach Artificial Reef

The Huntington Beach artificial reef was built in 1963. It consists of four separate
 A, B, C, and D. Each has three or four rock piles consisting of 1000 tons of quarry
. It covers a total of almost 4 acres and is fairly low relief, about 2 feet for most of
iles. It rests in 60 feet of water at the following locations:

Reef A
1. 33° 36.917' N x 117° 58.850' W
2. 33° 36.867' N x 117° 58.817' W
3. 33° 36.833' N x 117° 58.800' W
4. 33° 36.817' N x 117° 58.783' W
Reef B
1. 33° 37.167' N x 117° 59.300' W
2. 33° 37.150' N x 117° 59.283' W
3. 33° 37.117' N x 117° 59.267' W
Reef C
1. 33° 37.300' N x 117° 59.867' W
2. 33° 37.283' N x 117° 59.850' W
3. 33° 37.250' N x 117° 59.833' W

Reef D
1. 33° 37.483' N x 118° 00.083' W
2. 33° 37.467' N x 118° 00.067' W
3. 33° 37.433' N x 118° 00.050' W
4. 33° 37.400' N x 118° 00.033' W

The Huntington Beach Artificial reef is not nearly as good a fishing spot as the Bolsa
 reef but still has its moments. There are mostly Perch and Croakers here, though
ionally, the Barred Sand Bass action can get good. Some Sculpin and Halibut inhabit
ea as well. The best tactics are to fish the in-between flats with bait or artificials.

Newport Beach Artificial Reef

Originally built in 1979, the Newport Beach artificial reef was added to in 19[?] 1982 and 1984 and now covers about 8 acres. Over 10,000 tons of concrete rubble old pier pilings were used in its construction. It lies in 72 feet of water about 3½ miles Newport Beach in four different piles at:

33° 36.133' N x 117° 57.867' W
33° 36.267' N x 117° 57.733' W
33° 36.217' N x 117° 57.833' W
33° 36.117' N x 117° 57.883' W

The Newport Beach artificial reef is heavily populated with Perch and Blacksn[?] In the spring it has a pretty good Sculpin bite and in the summer, Barred Sand bass f to the area. Sometimes, Barracuda move through the area as well and the occasi[?] Yellowtail may be enticed to bite during the warmer summer months.

Foss 125

The Foss 125 is a 130 foot long steel barge. The Foss Launch and Tug com[?] operates all up and down the Pacific coast hauling lumber, oil and other commodities between the Pacific Northwest and Southern California. The Foss 125 sank in bad weather in 1958 and ended up off Laguna Beach. The Foss 125 lies in only 55 feet of water at:

33° 32.16' N x 117° 46.96' W

The Foss 125 is a pretty good fish attractant, enticing Perch, Calico Bass, Whitefish, Sculpin, and some Sheepshead to its undersea haven. It is fishable only during calm weather since it's fairly close to the surf line. Anchor up-current from the wreck and pay out anchor line until the boat is positioned over the wreck for best results.

Divers often call this the Cleo Street wreck because it lies just offshore of the beach access area at the foot of Cleo Street in Laguna Beach. It's about 150 yards directly offshore (230 degrees) from the stairway that provides beach access. It one of the few wrecks you can dive from shore. The visibility is often good and since the wreck is fairly shal-

*Patroling the flats surrounding artificial reefs [?]
wrecks, is the domain of the California Halibut[?]
This big bruiser was hauled up from just such[?]
place. There's some fine eating!*

, it's usually well lit. Though it is a barge, so has few spectacular features, it is, nonethe-
, a popular dive spot due to its convenience.

ditional Wrecks in Orange County

Following is the database for wrecks in this area. They're arranged from North to
ıth by wreck location:

Name	Type	Sunk	Reason	Tons	Coords	
:holas Biddle	Bark	1876	Stranded		33° 44.08' N	118° 05.70' W
known					33° 44.00' N	118° 07.50' W
‹	Schooner	1930		343	33° 43.58' N	118° 07.25' W
anna Smith	Steam screw	1935	Burned	3648	33° 43.58' N	118° 08.58' W
ie II	Barge	1956		85	33° 40.00' N	118° 02.00' W
tie Carson	Schooner	1881		286	33° 40.00' N	118° 05.00' W
:helor Boy	Gas screw	1923		45	33° 38.00' N	118° 03.00' W
e #1	Barge	1951	Foundered	79	33° 38.00' N	118° 04.00' W
known	Wreckage				33° 37.00' N	118° 13.00' W
‹ #2	Barge	1934	Burned	73	33° 37.00' N	118° 01.00' W
›ra	Schooner	1872	Stranded		33° 36.50' N	117° 55.83' W
agon	Oil yawl	1939	Stranded	176	33° 36.50' N	117° 54.25' W
ıer Buhne	Schooner	1927	Stranded	287	33° 36.50' N	117° 55.83' W
		1942			33° 36.00' N	117° 54.25' W
rs Truly	Gas yawl	1934	Burned	51	33° 36.00' N	117° 54.25' W
iel	Schooner barge	1925	Stranded	537	33° 36.00' N	117° 54.00' W
ıno	Schooner	1871	Stranded		33° 35.50' N	117° 52.70' W
ajo	Oil screw	1963		55	33° 35.00' N	118° 10.00' W
›r Wave	Gas schooner	1936	Wrecked		33° 35.00' N	117° 54.00' W
nown	Aircraft				33° 35.00' N	118° 05.00' W
nond	Steam screw	1926	Collision	650	33° 33.58' N	118° 00.00' W
rles Brown	Barge	1932	Stranded	72	33° 32.50' N	117° 47.00' W
nown	Aircraft				33° 32.00' N	117° 47.00' W
›aloma		1943	Wrecked		33° 32.00' N	117° 47.00' W
kee Boy		1950	Wrecked		33° 32.00' N	117° 49.00' W
; #125	Scow	1958		432	33° 32.00' N	117° 47.00' W
'ic Star		1941	Wrecked		33° 32.00' N	117° 48.00' W
ınie Boy	Oil screw	1950	Burned	85	33° 32.00' N	117° 47.00' W
ie Fjord	Schooner	1942		261	33° 30.00' N	118° 13.00' W
ıown	Japanese aircraft				33° 30.00' N	117° 45.00' W
Rex	Oil screw	1952	Foundered	113	33° 29.00' N	117° 47.00' W
ie	Oil screw	1965		194	33° 28.00' N	118° 00.00' W
#1	Barge	1948	Foundered	96	33° 27.67' N	117° 45.83' W
Saturnia	Screw MS	1955	Foundered	116	33° 27.00' N	117° 44.00' W
m		1940	Wrecked		33° 25.00' N	117° 37.00' W
:ern Pilot	Oil screw	1953	Burned	113	33° 22.00' N	117° 45.18' W
a	Barge	1936	Foundered	53	33° 05.00' N	118° 35.00' W

Ships are sunk for all sorts of reasons. Naval gunnery practice is just one of them. Here the USS Missour Mighty Mo, on whose decks the peace treaty with Japan ending WWII was signed, and also the ship firing opening shots of Desert Storm, unleashes the pyrotechnic fury of her 16 inch guns. Woe be to any ship or target on the receiving end of this onslaught.

Chapter 8
Northern San Diego County

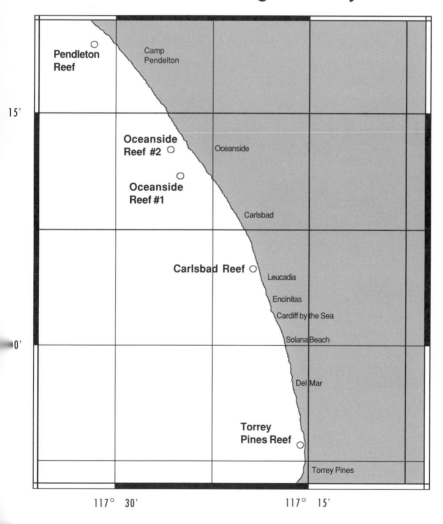

North County San Diego is blessed with some of the best coastal fishing on all the ~rnia Coast. This is enhanced even more by an abundance of artificial reefs built by ~lifornia Department of Fish and Game.

Pendleton Artificial Reef

The artificial reef just offshore of the Marine base at Camp Pendelton was buil 1980 with 10,000 tons of quarry rock. It lies in 43 feet of water and covers about 3 acres of sea bottom. The reef itself is comprised of eight closely clustered rock piles v a fairly large relief, some piles reaching 5 feet high or so. The center of the rockpile clus is located:

33° 19.500' N x 117° 31.700' W

The Pendleton artificial reef is an excellent fishing hole. Sand Bass cluster around between the structure during the summer months and Calico Bass are also found h year round, in good numbers. The reef grows a kelp canopy so all different specie surface fish can be caught here in the warmer weather including Yellowtail, Barracuda Bonito. This reef also get's its share of White Sea Bass, Sheepshead, and Perch. In al excellent, year round, hot spot.

Oceanside Reef #2

The second reef built in the sandy flats off the coast of the city of Ocean Oceanside #2 is a large, complex reef structure covering over 250 acres of sea floc was built in 1987 of 10,000 tons of quarry rock arranged in 3 rows of 4 rock piles

for a total of 12 separate rock piles. The water depth is from 45 to 75 feet. The GPS targets to find the reefs are:

1A. 33° 12.017' N x 117° 26.088' W
2A. 33° 12.347' N x 117° 26.068' W
3A. 33° 12.408' N x 117° 26.177' W
4A. 33° 12.527' N x 117° 26.242' W
1B. 33° 12.408' N x 117° 25.658' W
2B. 33° 12.523' N x 117° 25.772' W
3B. 33° 12.622' N x 117° 25.880' W
4B. 33° 12.738' N x 117° 25.943' W
1C. 33° 12.720' N x 117° 25.163' W
2C. 33° 12.797' N x 117° 25.227' W
3C. 33° 12.910' N x 117° 25.307' W
4C. 33° 13.050' N x 117° 25.402' W

The Oceanside reef #2 is another ex-cellent fishing spot. It collects more flats fish, such as Sand Bass and Halibut than the more condensed reefs like Pendelton. Nonethe-less, surface fishing at Oceanside #2 is often excellent, especially when the Barracuda run in the late spring and early summer. Yellow-tail are also caught here in the warmer sum-

In the warmer months, pelagic fish like thi Barracda visit shipwrecks and artificial reefs feed on the plentiful sea life they attract.

56

r months. Best bet is to fish the bottom unless you see birds diving on bait. This means face fish are driving the bait to the surface, a common sight over this and other artificial fs in the summer months.

eanside Reef #1

Just south of the bigger Oceanside reef #2, lies reef #1 in about 90 feet of water. ginally, 2000 tons or quarry rock were dumped on a 4 acre site in 1964. This was mented in 1987 with the addition of many concrete dock floats scattered about a 64 e area. This perked up the original site as a fish attractant and has now turned it into te a fishing hole. The center of the reef complex lies about 1 3/4 miles from the ance to Oceanside harbor on a 202° magnetic course at:

33° 10.950' N x 117° 25.000' W

There are 8 individual targets in the reef complex located at:

A - 33° 10.983' N x 117° 25.017' W
B - 33° 11.000' N x 117° 24.983' W
C - 33° 10.967' N x 117° 25.017' W
D - 33° 10.983' N x 117° 24.985' W
E - 33° 10.950' N x 117° 25.035' W
F - 33° 10.950' N x 117° 24.980' W
G - 33° 10.917' N x 117° 25.016' W
H - 33° 10.900' N x 117° 24.984' W

Barred Sandbass congregate in this area to spawn in the late spring and early sum-
Sheepshead, Sculpin and Perch are year round denizens of the reefs, and Halibut
ol the sandy bottom between the rock piles. At certain times of the year, Calico Bass
sometimes surface fish patrol the area during the appropriate seasons. Divers should
that Spiny Lobsters are commonly seen here during the winter months.

sbad Artificial Reef

The Carlsbad artificial reef was built in 1991. At that time, the Batiquitos Lagoon,
ntrance long silted in, was opened to tidal action to bring back habitat for many
tidal species. The wetlands serve as a nursery for these fish. When these fish grow to
ile size, they often wander into the open sea and right into the mouths of waiting
tory fish. Having a series of artificial reefs near the entrance of the lagoon, serves as
r for the fish, so they end up having a much better chance of becoming adult fish,
r than simply lunch.

The reef was built of about 10,000 tons of quarry rock, distributed in 12 separate
covering about 6 acres. The depth varies from about 35 feet to about 65 feet. It's
ed 6 miles from the Oceanside Harbor entrance on a 180° magnetic heading with the
r at:

33° 05.000' N x 117° 19.150' W

The 12 separate rock piles are located at:

A - 33° 05.325' N x 117° 19.218' W
B - 33° 05.235' N x 117° 19.183' W
C - 33° 05.163' N x 117° 19.153' W
D - 33° 05.058' N x 117° 19.122' W
E - 33° 05.280' N x 117° 19.240' W
F - 33° 05.190' N x 117° 19.220' W
G - 33° 05.090' N x 117° 19.190' W
H - 33° 05.000' N x 117° 19.150' W
I - 33° 05.260' N x 117° 19.420' W
J - 33° 05.180' N x 117° 19.380' W
K - 33° 05.080' N x 117° 19.340' W
L - 33° 04.970' N x 117° 19.320' W

Like other close to shore reefs, the Carlsbad reef isn't the best for surface fish
bigger reef fish, but it does attract many of the flats fish. The 30 foot depths are
preferred haunts for big Halibut, and the mouths of estuaries are the perfect hun
grounds for these ambush feeders. Sand Bass are also a staple of this reef.

Torrey Pines Artificial Reef #2
This Torrey Pines reef was built in 1975 of 3000 tons of quarry rock dropped
the 45 foot deep, sandy bottom ocean about 3 miles North (359 Magnetic) from the F
La Jolla tower. Concrete dock floats were added to the reef in 1979 to augment it
now a single pile of rocks covering about 1 acre with its center located at:

Calico Bass and Sheepshead congregating in a wreck

32° 53.583' N x 117° 15.590' W

Since this is a single rock pile with higher relief than many of the multiple pile reefs, reef tends to get a strong stand of kelp growing on it and supports strong popula- is of reef species like Calico Bass, Sheepshead, Blacksmith and Halfmoons. It's not essarily a good flats fish area, though the area around the reef is better than just a wide anse of hard bottom.

rey Pines Artificial Reef #1

This reef was built in 1964 of 1000 tons of quarry rock in 3 separate piles. It is h older and less developed that the later Torrey Pines Artificial Reef (#2.) It is in 67 of water about 2 ½ miles from the Point La Jolla tower on a 352 magnetic heading. approximate center of the piles lies at:

32° 53.200' N x 117° 15.830' W

Since its construction, there has been no maintenance nor augmentation of the reef, over the past nearly 40 years, sand and silt deposits have reduced the relief to being ly recognizable. It's not much of a fishing spot and not worth the dive. There are ly too many other fabulous spots to dive near La Jolla. The flats species inhabit the , but it wouldn't be worth the effort to seek out this reef, over many of the other fine ng spots in the vicinity.

itional Wrecks in Northern San Diego County

Following is the database for wrecks in this area. They're arranged from North to h by wreck location:

Northern San Diego County					
Name	Type	Sunk	Reason	Tons	Coordinates
¡ger	Oil screw	1948	Foundered	90	33° 22.00' N 117° 37.50' W
ain	Oil screw	1951	Foundered	14	33° 12.17' N 117° 23.83' W
¡ector	Oil screw	1930	Burned	78	33° 11.00' N 117° 22.75' W
Home II	Oil screw	1956		65	33° 11.00' N 117° 24.00' W
¨ Co. #1		1933	Wrecked		33° 11.00' N 117° 22.75' W
¡oop #1	Barge	1928	Foundered	58	33° 10.00' N 117° 22.17' W
¡ge W Hind	Bark	1936	Foundered	1389	33° 09.00' N 117° 22.00' W
¡ad		1943			33° 09.00' N 117° 21.00' W
¨		1945			33° 09.00' N 117° 21.00' W
¡Mayne	Barge	1939	Foundered	431	33° 07.67' N 117° 20.00' W
¡V	Oil screw	1952	Foundered	50	32° 59.00' N 117° 26.00' W
¡eorge	Oil screw	1954	Foundered	214	32° 52.00' N 117° 50.00' W
	Steamship	1915			32° 51.00' N 117° 17.00' W
¡	Gas screw	1924		41	32° 50.00' N 117° 19.00' W
¡r	Oil screw	1950	Foundered	56	32° 50.00' N 117° 17.00' W
¡Markham	Oil screw	1957		79	32° 50.00' N 117° 17.00' W

Schools of fish often teem all over shipwrecks and artificial reefs

Chapter 9
Southern San Diego County

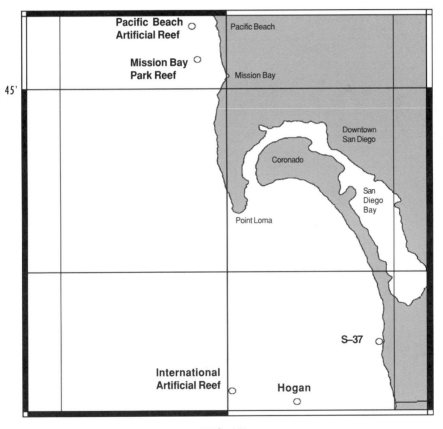

With a major harbor, an excellent second harbor ideal for yachts, artificial reefs, wrecks and the famous "Wreck Alley" of scuttled ships for the sole purpose of ng fishermen and divers, Southern San Diego County has it all for the fisherman or . Few places, anywhere on earth, can compare with the wide variety of marine facili- nd attractions that San Diego boasts. In addition, San Diego has an incredible fleet of

open party, charter and long range fishing and diving boats available to the fishermen o
diver without his own.

Pacific Beach Artificial Reef

The Pacific Beach Artificial Reef was built in 1987 with 10,000 tons of quarry roc
in 42 to 72 feet of water about a mile off the coast of Pacific Beach. It consists of 1
separate rock piles arranged in three rows of four piles each covering about 100 acre
The GPS targets to find these rock piles are:

1A. 32° 47.333' N x 117° 16.700' W
2A. 32° 47.417' N x 117° 16.750' W
3A. 32° 47.583' N x 117° 16.833' W
4A. 32° 47.667' N x 117° 16.917' W
1B. 32° 47.400' N x 117° 16.500' W
2B. 32° 47.500' N x 117° 16.500' W
3B. 32° 47.633' N x 117° 16.567' W
4B. 32° 47.933' N x 117° 16.583' W
1C. 32° 47.500' N x 117° 16.200' W
2C. 32° 47.600' N x 117° 16.200' W
3C. 32° 47.733' N x 117° 16.233' W
4C. 32° 47.833' N x 117° 16.300' W

The Pacific Beach reef is Bass heaven. Both Calicos and Sand Bass inhabit the ar
in excellent numbers. Also around the reef other flats fish congregate to get in on t
action such as Sculpin, Halibut and a few others. There's usually not much surface actic
around this reef, though. It's primarily a bottom fishing proposition.

Mission Bay Park Artificial Reef

Often called "Wreck Alley" by fishermen and divers, the Mission Bay Park arti
cial reef consists of a number of different wrecks and reefs. Originally, a reef of co

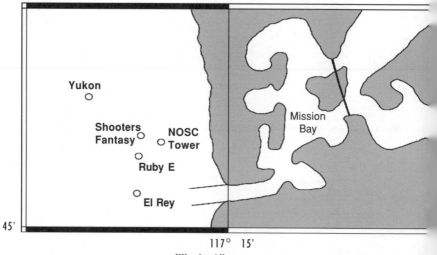

Wreck Alley

62

rubble was planned, but then, through the great work of the San Diego Oceans
dation, some magical things began to happen. Donated ships were scuttled there
ing an underwater park unlike anything that had ever been seen before. A Navy
ated oceanographic tower was on the site and then collapsed in a storm creating yet
ner fabulous element to the mix

y E

The Ruby E began life as a Coast Guard Cutter named the Cyane. This was a 165'
Class Patrol Boat. It was built in 1934 and served in the Gulf of Alaska in the late
s. When WWII broke out, the Coast Guard sprang into action and armed their
rs more heavily with depth charge racks and rocket launchers to augment their deck
The Cyane was then designated WPC-105 and served bravely in the Aleutian Cam-
.

The Coast Guard retired this ship in 1950 and auctioned it off in 1954. It was
erted to a fishing boat, then again to a salvage vessel, and its name changed to the
E. After being repossessed and sold a number of other times, the owners decided
rap the vessel, so they removed anything of value and donated the hulk to be added
ission Bay's "wreck alley" artificial reef. In 1989, the ship went on it's final mission to
ottom in 90 feet of water. It lies at:

$$32° 46.033' N x 117° 16.600' W$$

The wreck itself is extremely easy to spot from the surface since it is marked with a
w Department of Fish and Game buoy. This buoy is attached to the bow of the ship.
Diving the Ruby E is a very exciting experience. The visibility is often excellent, the
complete and upright, and is covered with all manner of marine life. Beware the

The Cyane, the The Ruby E when it was doing its duty as a Coast Guard Cutter.

y boat traffic in the area, however. The seas have been taking their toll on the wreck so
s should beware of the sharp rusty metal all around. Penetration should only be
pted by those who are properly trained and rated for this kind of dive. Getting

trapped in the hull whan something goes wrong has little margin for error.

El Rey

The El Rey was a kelp harvesting vessel. Built in the 1950s, the sturdy vessel spent it's entire career in Southern California harvesting kelp, used in the manufacture of foods, pharmaceuticals and fertilizer. When the ship was retired in the 1980s, it was donated to the Department of Fish and Game to be used in the wreck alley artificial reef. Any fuel, oil or other environmentally unfriendly equipment was removed from the ship, holes were cut into the deck to allow access by scuba divers, then a Navy demolitions team blew a big hole in the hull, sending the El Rey to the bottom. It now lies in 75 feet of water at:

A diver emerges from a hatch on the Ruby E

32°32° 45.850' N x 117° 16.633' W

The El Rey also has a yellow buoy attached to it, and this is the best way to locat wreck.

The El Rey sits upright, so is a great dive spot. The erosive nature of the sea is qu disintegrating the ship, and many of the inner spaces, once considered fairly safe to etrate, are now collapsed. The steel hull has buckled and sharp protrusions abound. now unsafe to penetrate, but makes a fascinating dive to view underwater. Normall visibility isn't the best, 10-20 feet, but on calm mornings, especially in the winter, it c excellent. All manner of sea life, you might expect on a reef, await the diver interest underwater flora and fauna.

Shooters Fantasy

The Shooters Fantasy was a 65 foot steel sportfishing boat operated out of Diego in the 1960s and 70s. It was retired and donated to the San Diego Oceans fou tion, then scuttled in the Mission Bay "wreck alley" park in 1987. It now lies at:

32° 46.233' N x 117° 16.300' W

NOSC Tower

The Naval Ocean Systems Center, in San Diego built this tower in 1959 to s shallow sea water behavior and science. Waves, currents, underwater acoustics, tem ture gradients and all manner of oceanographic science were studied here throughou 1960s and 1970s. Even new theories in equipment design were tested out here b being approved for on-ship testing. The tower's contribution to the Navy's oceanogr

Diver Helios Gonzales poses next to one of the El Rey's props.

wledge base was extensive.

By the mid 1980s, the tower's usefulness was marginal, and the Navy decided they
ld do everything the tower could do easier and cheaper, so they donated the tower to

Scripps Institute of Oceanography in
5. Scripps only had the tower for a little
e than a year, when in a violent storm in
ary 1988, the aging structure collapsed
the sea while being pommeled by sav-
seas. It now lies in 70 feet of water just
Mission Beach at:

32°32° 46.367' N x 117° 16.067' W

To the diver approaching the NOSC
r, the structure appears as a jumble of
kage. There is little recognizable form
e rubble. For this reason it is consid-
unsafe to penetrate anywhere. A con-
able amount of marine plants and ani-
now have become a part of the wreck-
nd their continual interaction makes this

a fascinating place to study. Visibility is occasionally a problem, especially in the afternoo
when choppy surges and wave action stirs up the silty bottom, cutting visibility down
dismal.

Yukon

The Yukon is the latest addition to "Wreck Alley." It is a Canadian destroyer, 366 f
long, donated to the San Diego Oceans Foundation. It was built in 1961 and served
Canadian Navy diligently from its launching until 1987, when it was retired. It is interest
to note that of the four McKenzie class destroyers built (Mackenzie, Saskatchewan, Yuk
and Qu'Appelle) three are now artificial reefs, two off the British Colombia coast and
Yukon in San Diego. The fourth, the Qu'Appelle, was scrapped in 1992. These ships w
named after major rivers in Canada.

The Yukon was towed to San Diego and prepped for the scuttling by removing
equipment that may have held oil or fuel, then holes were cut in various places in the l
to allow divers to have access into the hull. The ship was towed into position and exp
sives packed in critical areas of the hull to make sure water entered the hull evenly, and
ship would sink upright. Before the explosive charges could be detonated, the rocking

The complex structure of the NOSC Tower attracts many different fish

the ship by the swells the night before its appointed date with destiny, allowed seawat
flood the hull, sending it to the bottom prematurely and not so level. The ship's
buried into sea first and it rolled over on its port side, settling onto the sand below w
rather severe port list. It now lies in water from 55 to 100 feet deep at:

The Yukon as it appeared in Canadian Navy service

The Yukon is a very popular dive site. The location, only minutes from the channel
rance at Mission Bay, makes it readily accessible from small boats, though it is too far
hore to reach from the beach. It is also a fresh wreck, so very recognizable underwa-

One of the Yukon's forward guns now silenced by the sea.

ter. The visibility in this area can be good, sometimes 75 feet or more. Though the ship penetrable by experienced divers, the many narrow passageways and low ceilings typic of warships, makes penetrating the wreck an activity only for those who know wr they're doing.

The "Wreck Alley" area has always been a good flats fishing area, even before t ships were sunk on he site. The addition of the reefs has only improved the area f Halibut and Sand Bass. In addition, surface fish tend to congregate around the area. B and Barracuda, especially, enjoy life around these reefs, along with the occasional Yello tail during the season.

S-37

Built in 1918 at the close of WWI, the Submarine S-37 wasn't commissioned ur 1923. It served in the Pacific fleet in the Philippines between the wars, and when WV broke out, it fought in Southeast Asia from the Philippines to Australia, sinking seve Japanese transports and warships. The old boat was tired, though, and continual mecha cal and electrical problems plagued the boat so it was taken back to San Diego in 19 The Navy stripped the boat and was towing it out to sea to be used as a bombing tar when the towline broke and the boat foundered and sank in 50 feet of water, just Imperial Beach. The S-37 is a popular sport diving spot and lies:

32° 34.633' N x 117° 8.000' W

Be careful, when approaching the wreck. The conning tower is sometimes aw during low tides and often, waves break over the boat. Treat it as you would a boiler r and make sure you use caution when approaching. The area around the boat has v good flats fishing with Halibut and Sand Bass frequenting the area in very good numb Croakers, as you might find surf fishing, and Perch are also common at the submari

The first impression of most divers when they see the S-37 is that it couldn't l submarine - it's just too small. Well, in WWI, when this sub was built, those things v tiny! The silty bottom in the area and proximity of the wreck to shore makes the visib

The S-37 douing its duty between the World Wars

ierally poor. Though some well qualified divers do penetrate the hull on occasion, the
remely cramped space and poor visibility make it a dive only for experts. It is danger-
; to enter. Exploring the exterior, though can be interesting on days when the water isn't
› murky. The hull has been growing a substantial colony of mussels in recent years. The
:ck is too far offshore to be easily reached from the beach, so a boat is the only way to
t it.

›gan

The Hogan is a Navy destroyer built in 1919 in San Francisco. It was assigned to
ific duty and served on both the coasts of California and Hawaii until 1922 when it
. decommissioned and laid up until 1940. It was re-commissioned as a high speed
ie sweeper, as the clouds of war spread across Europe. Like many of the older de-
›yers early in the war, the Hogan escorted convoys of cargo ships crossing the North
intic, protecting them from marauding German submarines. The ship took part in the
:ed landing in North Africa in 1942, the Marshall Islands, Saipan, Tinian and Iwo Jima
944, and early 1945, then returned to San Diego. It was used as a bombing target in
vember of 1945 and sunk at these co-ordinates:

32° 32.283' N x 117° 12.083' W

The Hogan gets its share of reef fish, even getting some Ling Cod in the winter
iths and White Seabass in the spring. It's also a good Perch, and sometimes Sheeps-
d habitat. Often good numbers of Calico Bass surround the wreck as do Sand Bass in
flats areas surrounding the hulk. It's worth a stop if you're in the area to see what might
round.

*A Blue Shark cruises by as divers descend to a wreck. Though potentially dangerous, blues are rarely
agressive and are more curious than anything else - but they sure can surprise you underwater.*

69

Many divers consider diving on the Hogan to be the best wreck dive in the S Diego area. It sits in 125 to 130 feet of water, so is considered an expert dive only. T stern section is fairly intact with the propellors and shafts still attached. The center secti has collapsed into a jumble of machinery, plumbing and structure. The bow lies ups down and has collapsed into a low relief. This site often has excellent visibility.

International Artificial Reef

It is called the International Artificial Reef because it is situated just this side of international border between the US and Mexico. This reef is the newest and deepest all of the manmade artificial reefs. It came into being when a Trident Missile testing to collapsed in 1992. It has been added to since, with the addition of 10,000 tons of qua rock and 3,000 tons of concrete rubble. It's still under construction and covers over acres of sea floor in six distinct piles. They lie in 165 feet of water at:

1. 32° 32.672' N x 117° 14.885' W
2. 32° 32.662' N x 117° 14.900' W
3. 32° 32.625' N x 117° 14.833' W
4. 32° 32.647' N x 117° 14.803' W
5. 32° 32.717' N x 117° 14.842' W
Tower: 32° 32.495' N x 117° 14.790' W

The International Reef has everything - excellent reef fish fishing including R Cod, Sheepshead, Perch and others, very good flats fishing around the reef for Sand B Halibut, Sculpin and other flats fish. In the warmer months, it has good surface fishin the warmer months. A few years ago, in an El Niño year, six pack charter boats use troll the area for a school of huge bonito, bigger than most Yellowtail that year, righ this spot.

The Hogan, as it appeared in WWII, fought bravely during the war in spite of its age. It now sits on the bottom off Imperial Beach and attracts fish

Considered too deep to dive, many were quite shocked to see photographs of ers amongst the wreckage of the missile launch platform published on the Internet. ese divers were using special inert gas mixtures to dive to this depth. It is too deep for rt divers to approach, so don't even think about it unless you're a trained and experi-ed expert diver.

ditional Wrecks in Southern San Diego County

Following is the database for wrecks in this area. They're arranged from North to ith by wreck location:

"Scattered wreckage" means just that, as this diver has discovered.

Southern San Diego County

Name	Type	Sunk	Reason	Tons	Coordinates	
Capistrano		1911	Wrecked		32° 46.50' N	117° 15.00'
El Rey	Kelp harvester	1987	Scuttled	100	32° 46.23' N	117° 16.30'
Shooters Fantasy	Sport Fisherman	1987	Scuttled		32° 46.23' N	117° 16.30'
Strider	Sailing yacht	1987	Scuttled	36	32° 46.23' N	117° 16.30'
Ruby E	Cutter	1987	Scuttled	165	32° 46.23' N	117° 16.30'
Shoshoni	Oil screw	1965	Burned	55	32° 46.00' N	117° 14.50'
Dot		1951	Capsized		32° 45.42' N	117° 15.50'
Lazy Days	Barge	1953	Foundered	93	32° 44.00' N	117° 16.33'
Radio	Schooner	1950	Foundered	137	32° 43.50' N	117° 12.50'
Sea Products #3	Barge	1931	Wrecked	83	32° 42.50' N	117° 11.00'
Alaskan		1910			32° 42.50' N	117° 11.00'
Mondego	Oil screw	1967		306	32° 42.00' N	117° 10.00
Fanny		1851	Capsized		32° 41.13' N	117° 13.92
Belgian King	Steamship	1899	Stranded		32° 41.13' N	117° 13.92
Olympic	Barkentine	1948		1469	32° 41.00' N	117° 15.50
Diana		1948			32° 41.00' N	117° 15.00
Tryst	Oil screw	1976	Stranded	12	32° 40.93' N	117° 12.93
New World	Oil screw	1945	Foundered	55	32° 40.83' N	117° 11.50
Bohemia	Steam screw	1931	Wrecked	1633	32° 40.00' N	117° 13.00
Penelope	Schooner	1922			32° 40.00' N	117° 20.00
Lovely Flora	Schooner	1858	Stranded		32° 40.00' N	117° 15.00
Narwhale	Bark	1934		523	32° 40.00' N	117° 10.00
Kelpie	Schooner	1926			32° 40.00' N	117° 20.00
Northern Light	Tuna clipper	1955	Explosion & fire		32° 40.00' N	117° 17.00
Dorothy Phillips		1941			32° 40.00' N	117° 15.00
Despatch #5	Gas screw	1926	Stranded	59	32° 40.00' N	117° 14.67
Aliciel	Gas screw	1916	Stranded	709	32° 40.00' N	117° 14.00
Aquarius	Oil screw	1980	Foundered	49	32° 39.90' N	117° 14.50
Plutus	Schooner	1858	Stranded		32° 39.75' N	117° 14.50
Glendale	Schooner	1930		296	32° 39.67' N	117° 14.50
Pacific		1922			32° 39.67' N	117° 14.50
Idaho (Y P 198)	Gas screw	1943	Wrecked	22	32° 39.67' N	117° 14.50
Sachtleben	Oil screw	1940	Grounded	57	32° 39.67' N	117° 14.50
Diablo (Dyablo)	Steam screw	1873	Wrecked	1451	32° 39.67' N	117° 14.50
Triton	Oil screw	1943	Stranded	12	32° 39.67' N	117° 14.50
Finita		1954	Collision		32° 39.00' N	117° 15.00
Sea Hawk	Oil screw	1945	Collision	83	32° 38.50' N	117° 15.00
Mildura II	Oil yacht	1932	Stranded	47	32° 38.50' N	117° 15.00
Mindanao	Schooner	1946	Wrecked	566	32° 38.50' N	117° 15.00
Monte Carlo	Tanker	1936	Stranded	2702	32° 38.15' N	117° 08.1
High Seas	Purse seiner	1970		392	32° 37.00' N	117° 12.5
F #1	Submarine	1917	Collision	330	32° 37.00' N	117° 15.0
PC 815	Subchaser	1945	Wrecked		32° 36.00' N	117° 18.0
YC 689	Subchaser	1943	Grounded		32° 35.83' N	117° 08.1
Mohican	Bark	1926	Wrecked	852	32° 35.00' N	117° 20.0
W R Chamberlin Jr.		1941			32° 35.00' N	117° 20.0
S-37	Submarine	1945	Parted tow		32° 34.63' N	117° 08.0
Hogan	Destroyer	1945	bombing target		32° 32.28' N	117° 12.0
Belle Isle	Screw Ferry	1934	Foundered	169	32° 30.00' N	117° 14.0
Admiral	Oil screw	1949	Foundered	26	32° 15.00' N	117° 35.0

Chapter 10
Santa Catalina Island

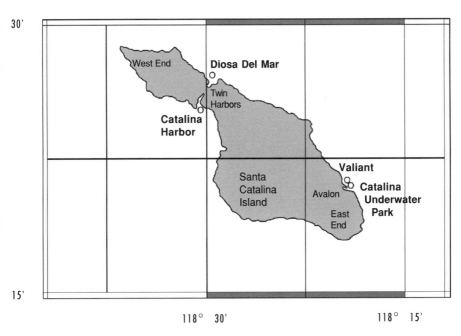

Santa Catalina Island, or simply, Catalina, lies only a couple dozen miles off the coast
southern California. It is Southern California's boaters', divers', and fishermen's play-
nd. It offers fabulous scenery, protected coves, great diving, excellent fishing and, in
ral, a little paradise only a short hop from the hustle and bustle of the huge metropolis
makes up most of Southern California's coastline. In addition to watersports, Calalina
has camping, hiking, rock climbing, and all the activities a ground based outdoor
likes, as well. Catalina also has shipwrecks, just waiting for the interested diver to
re.

Catalina Underwater Park

While not a fishing spot, the Catalina Underwater Park, sometimes referred to as Casino Point Underwater Park, is a diver's dream. There is just about every kind of sea environment found in California, all in one small area, with handy steps into the wa from the beach. There are shallow reefs, deep reefs, cliffs, caves, sandy bottoms and, shipwrecks - quite a few of them, all for the enjoyment of scuba and snorkel divers. I sunken boats, plus wreckage from a swimming platform, an old pier and several ma engines can be viewed underwater. The protected nature of the area and crystal c waters of Catalina Island make this the perfect place for divers to discover the fascina world of wreck diving.

Note - within this park you may take nothing - not fish, shellfish nor wreck sou nirs. Leave everything exactly as you found it.

At the South end of the park, the schooner Sujac is the first main wreck. IT is an long ferro-cement hulled gaff rigged schooner. In 1980, during a fierce Santa Ana w condition, she was riding out the storm well, anchored just outside the Avalon Chan entrance, when the anchor started dragging, taking her directly in toward the breakwa The crew jumped in the water to safety and were picked up by the Avalon Harbor Pa but the hull smashed into the jagged breakwater, opening a huge hole. The boat slid ur

settling on the bottom in 75 feet of water. It has been salvaged since and only the bare hull remains.

North of the Sujac, lies a small sail boat, a glass bottomed boat that used to take tourists out of Avalon, and a sailboat called the Kismet. Farther up yet is a 27 foot sailboat called the Eleanor, some pilings from a pier that collapsed, and an old swim platform that sunk years ago.

Boats are kept out of the park with buoys and rope, but can approach quite closely. The best time to dive is in the winter when boat traffic is minimal.

The Valiant shipwreck, just North of the underwater park, is probably one of the most visited wrecks in all of Southern California. It was launched in 1926 as a 162 foot long luxury yacht named Aras, (the owner's wife spelled backward) It was sold to Charles Howard, now famous for being the man who owned and raced the thoroughbred

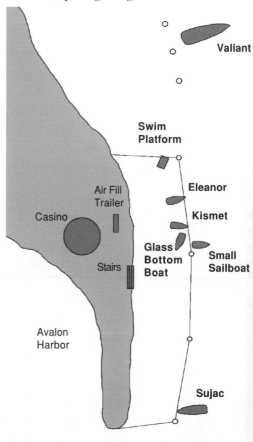

The Catalina (Casino Point) Underwater Park

horse, "Seabiscuit." He moved the ship to San Francisco the same year to tour the Pacific coast. While anchored in Descanso Bay and visiting Avalon, the main settlement on Catalina, the ship caught fire. The harbor master tried to tow the boat away from other anchored boats but the blazing fire kept burning the towline. Finally after burning for two days, the Valiant slipped beneath the waves to its final resting place.

The Kismet lying on its side in the Catalina Underwater Park

Though much of the shipwreck has been salvaged, it is now illegal to remove any-g from the wreck, so it quietly sits on the bottom serving to attract schools of Perch in clear Catalina waters. It rests on a sandy bottom in 80 feet of water at:

33° 21.416'N x 118° 19.333'W

The Valiant is primarily a Perch attractor with schools of Halfmoons, Blacksmith, Opaleyes constantly circling around and through the wreck. In addition, Calico Bass ıent the wreck and the sandy bottom surrounding the wreck attracts Halibut and r sand dwellers. The wreck is not fishable, though, because of its location amid the

The Valiant as it appeared during its short life as a luxury yacht, now a fish attracting wreck at Catalina Island

mooring buoys of Descanso Bay. Why would you want to anyway, with many even bet
fishing spots nearby.

The Valiant is often a new wreck diver's first actual wreck dive. It's perfect
cutting your teeth on this fascinating hobby. The Valiant sits on a sandy bottom with
stern in about 70 feet of water and the bow in about 100. It's in an area with clear wa
minimal currents and no surge, making it an ideal dive location. The bow and stern s
tions are very recognizable but the midship area has collapsed, partially from the fire t
caused its sinking in the first place and partly from the degradation of sitting submerge
seawater for all of these years. It is covered with colorful sea life. It's an easy shore dive
may be reached by boat, but be sure to obtain the required permit before taking
plunge.

It has been rumored that a considerable amount of jewelry and valuables have ne
been recovered from the wreck, but it is strictly forbidden to remove anything from
site. Quite a number of drink tokens were recovered in years past, but much of the ric
the wealthy passengers brought aboard is now gone forever.

*The Valiant's last gasp at life, as it slips slowly out of sight in Descanso Bay after burning
severly in a mysterious fire.*

Diosa Del Mar

This 90 foot schooner yacht, built in 1898 collided with Ship Rock just off
Isthmus area of Santa Catalina Island and went down in 1990. It's in a well traveled
popular spot, easily accessible for most smaller boats. The Diosa Del Mar raced
number of Newport to Ensenada races and was the first schooner to finish the ra
1979. It's owners sailed to Hawaii, explored the islands for several years and returne
Southern California in 1982. The Diosa Del Mar lies in about 25 feet of water at:

33° 27.800' N x 118° 29.395' W

This wreck site is almost always packed with Halfmoons, (Blue Perch) son
them going two pounds or more, but many are in the 8 or 10 inch range. It's also kr
as an excellent Calico Bass location and can harbor a wide variety of other reef dwe

ite Seabass also seem to favor this wreck. Breezing Yellowtail are also a common site
this area with bigger fish appearing in the warmer months when Spanish Mackerel
ear. Barracuda are also available here in-season and the usual rocky reef fish (Sheeps-
d and Whitefish) can also be found here in fishable numbers. Blacksmith Perch and
aleye are two other common visitors to this wreck and at times can be a nusance
ling the bait intended for bigger prey.

There are quite a few fabulous photographs of the wreck published both in print
on the Internet, of divers frolicking around a near complete and majestic appearing
ck. Rest assured, these photos were taken when the wreck was fresh. After all, it did
only a few years ago. Now, as this book is being published, 2004, it has been down
re for 14 years and you would be hard pressed to find much of the wreck remaining.
a dive site it is terrific, but more for the majestic rock and cliff formations, abundant
life and natural surroundings, rather than for observing the shipwreck.

alina Harbor

Catalina Harbor, Cat Harbor to the locals, sits on the back side of the island (when
ved from shore.) It's the only truly secure port on that side of the island from the
vailing north-westerly winds and swells. Cat Harbor is at the isthmus of the island
re the small town of Twin Harbors thrives. On the opposite side of the island, only a
hundred yards wide at that point, lies the other of the twin harbors, Isthmus Harbor.

Cat Harbor has been a favorite site
filming movies throughout the past
tury. In the 1920's and 1930's the
vie studios were pumping out hun-
ls of films, so so needed a good place
e-create exotic locales. The nearby, but
ote appearing, shoreline of Catalina
perfect for this so was used as all
s of unusual places, from the shores
Tripoli, to tropical isles, to the coast-
of Africa, Asia, the Carribean and
about anywhere else movie makers
at imagine.

In those days, Hollywood scoured
world to buy older sailing ships that
d be dressed up to appear as slavers,
te ships or whatever the movie called
then blown up and sent to Davy
s locker as the dashing hero swung
afety from a nearby hawser. Just a
of the many movies made at
lina included: Treasure Island, Old
sides, Sea Hawk and Mutiny on the
aty. The ships used for these adven-
films were often on their last legs

Sometimes wrecks offer up fabulous sport fish.
like this beautiful White Seabass

and no longer serviceable as commercial ships.

A number of the Hollywood Navy ships ended up on the bottom in Catalina H bor. While a couple of these ships were famous and well known, still others have alm no or very sketchy records on their origins and fates.

Ning Po

The Ning Po is one of the most famous ships in Cat Harbor. This was the ol wooden ship known to be afloat when it was anchored there. The Ning Po was a foot long Chinese Junk built in 1753 almost entirely of teak, camphor, and other ex woods. It was originally a cargo vessel, praised for its speed and maneuverability. Beca of its speed, it's use turned to smuggling and transporting slaves. In 1796, the ship ser as a war ship in the rebellion against the Chinese Emperor.

It was seized by the Chinese government in 1806 for smuggling and piracy and ag captured in 1814 when it was burned. Rebuilt, it again turned to smuggling, being sei once again, in 1823. Then it was confiscated by the British in 1834 to transport sl women to Canton. In 1841, it again was captured by the Chinese government an served as a prison ship for pirates and smugglers. It is said that when keeping the priso became too expensive, they were simply taken up on deck and beheaded - suppose 158 prisoners were killed in a single day.

In 1861 it was stolen by rebels and used as a transport, but then was again captu by the British. Back in Chinese hands, in Hong Kong, it served as a tour boat in the 1880s. Sometimes the passengers were robbed by the crew and set ashore on deserted islands. The British again captured the ship and resold it to Chinese owners. It was sold to Americans in 1911. After being damaged several times in typhoons, it was sailed to the West coast of the United States in 1912 and put on display in Venice, California. Then in 1915, it was towed to San Diego and put on display. About 1917 it was taken to Catalina

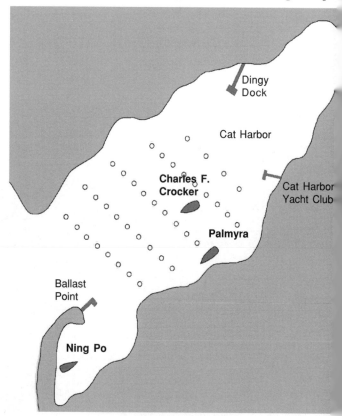

The wrecks of Catalina Harbor

ere it sat on anchor. In 1935, it was burned for a movie and the hulk sank into the
llow mud behind Ballast Point in Cat Harbor.

arles F. Crocker

The Charles F. Crocker was a 4 masted barkentine built in Alameda, California in
0. It was 204 feet long, 40 foot beam and displaced 762 tons. During its early career,
as used as a coastwise cargo ship ferrying lumber and manufactured goods between
thern California, Northern California, Washington and Oregon.

By the mid 1920's, sailing ships were simply no longer economically viable as com-
cial freight carriers. Steamships were more reliable, faster, could hold to schedules
er, and required a much smaller crew to operate. The smaller wooden ships like the
cker, were first to be culled from shipping companies' inventories. In 1927, the Charles
rocker was sold to Tom White for use in motion pictures.

In making a movie, the ship's masts were dynamited as it lay at anchor, since the
e called for a demasted ship. The movie hero was then rescued from its decks. Fol-
ng the movie the ship was just abandoned, partially aground in the shallow harbor. In
late 1930's the wreck was set afire. No one knows why - perhaps for a movie, perhaps
vandalism. Much of the hull disappeared, but the keel, ribs and bottom, sunk into the
l of Catalina. Later, in the 1950's, a major earthquake in South America sent a tidal
e into Cat Harbor sweeping clean any evidence of the Crocker from view.

The hulk was rediscovered several decades later on the bottom of the harbor in its
ent position. Divers can visit the wreck still between several moorings in 15-20 feet of
r. Wood beams and rows of brass hull spikes are about all that's left of this once
d ship.

nyra

The Palmyra is a ship surrounded in some mystery. It was a 75 foot long wooden
masted schooner. It was believed to have sunk for a movie in about 1938, but may
been part of the fire that eventually destroyed the Ning Po and the Charles F. Crocker,
aps that event, as well, was the backdrop for some forgotten film.

The tidal wave in the 1950s moved the Palmyra a considerable distance back into the
or from its original position. It now sits in shallow water amongst the moorings as
n in the diagram.

itional Wrecks near Catalina

Following is the database for wrecks in this area. They're arranged from North to
h by wreck location:

Catalina is the ideal place for divers to discover the fascination of wreck diving with clear water, minimal surge and lots of wrecks to explore.

Santa Catalina Island

Name	Type	Sunk	Reason	Tons	Coordinates	
V W #26	Scow	1943		60	33° 15.00' N	119° 30.00' W
inka		1939			33° 15.00' N	119° 30.00' W
e Ours		1943			33° 15.00' N	119° 30.00' W
Gironde	Schooner	1902		204	33° 15.00' N	119° 30.00' W
press		1942			33° 15.00' N	119° 30.00' W
lwing		1928	Wrecked		33° 15.00' N	118° 57.00' W
4431	Scow	1951		389	33° 15.00' N	119° 35.00' W
th Head	Oil screw	1954	Burned	50	33° 15.00' N	118° 15.00' W
th Star		1920			33° 16.00' N	118° 16.00' W
erican Rose	Oil screw	1952	Burned	120	33° 17.00' N	118° 54.50' W
8	Aircraft				33° 17.00' N	118° 19.00' W
dward	Oil yawl	1931	Burned	63	33° 17.00' N	118° 24.00' W
Sebastian	Galleon	1754			33° 18.00' N	118° 30.00' W
e Sky	Oil screw	1952	Wrecked	99	33° 18.00' N	118° 18.00' W
g #1	Scow	1925	Wrecked	285	33° 20.00' N	118° 18.00' W
thers	Scow	1941	Foundered	54	33° 20.00' N	118° 18.00' W
sino II	Gas yacht	1935		33	33° 20.00' N	118° 19.00' W
Co #12	Barge	1926	Wrecked	330	33° 20.00' N	118° 18.00' W
ta Rosa	Oil screw	1956			33° 21.00' N	118° 19.00' W
a		1933			33° 21.00' N	118° 19.00' W
nyra	Clipper	1908	Burned	1299	33° 21.00' N	118° 19.00' W
Timer	Oil screw	1966		81	33° 21.00' N	118° 19.00' W
y D	Oil screw	1953			33° 21.00' N	118° 19.00' W
fic	Oil screw	1951	Foundered	89	33° 21.00' N	117° 19.00' W
ant	Oil yawl	1930	Burned	444	33° 21.42' N	118° 19.33' W
vard	Oil screw	1950	Burned	51	33° 22.00' N	117° 45.30' W
n	Sloop	1891			33° 22.00' N	118° 25.00' W
dard II	Oil screw	1951			33° 22.00' N	119° 42.00' W
ephine		1832			33° 22.00' N	118° 25.00' W
press	Gas screw	1935		39	33° 22.00' N	118° 20.00' W
ire		1931			33° 22.00' N	118° 20.00' W
on		1949			33° 22.15' N	118° 25.00' W
oit	Gas screw	1932		43	33° 22.15' N	118° 25.00' W
ago	Oil screw	1943	Foundered	75	33° 23.00' N	118° 31.00' W
e		1954			33° 23.87' N	118° 21.98' W
ant		1932			33° 24.00' N	118° 21.00' W
am G Irwin	Bark	1926	Burned	348	33° 25.00' N	118° 30.00' W
Po	Chinese junk	1931	Old age	291	33° 25.00' N	118° 30.00' W
to		1937	Wrecked		33° 25.00' N	118° 20.00' W
ellyn J Morse	Ship	1926	Burned	1392	33° 25.00' N	118° 30.00' W
Co #9	Barge	1926	Wrecked	173	33° 25.00' N	118° 30.00' W
Co #8	Barge	1924	Wrecked	173	33° 25.00' N	118° 30.00' W
rica	Oil screw	1957		55	33° 25.00' N	118° 25.00' W
garet C	Schooner Barge	1933	Burned	58	33° 25.00' N	118° 30.00' W
ance	Schooner	1932		42	33° 25.00' N	118° 25.00' W
Tide					33° 25.80' N	118° 35.00' W
nty II	Ship				33° 26.00' N	118° 30.00' W
stra Senora de Ayuda	Galleon	1641		230	33° 26.00' N	118° 35.00' W
nown	Sailboat	1974			33° 26.00' N	118° 29.00' W
estic Swan	Schooner	1969			33° 26.00' N	118° 29.00' W
us	Schooner	1924	Burned	551	33° 27.00' N	118° 29.00' W
Alta	Oil yawl	1931	Burned	102	33° 27.00' N	118° 30.00' W
tus	Oil yacht	1936		48	33° 27.00' N	118° 17.00' W
ie Boy	Oil screw	1955	Burned	64	33° 27.00' N	118° 36.00' W
les F Crocker	Bark	1926	Foundered	860	33° 27.00' N	118° 30.00' W
Pedro	Galleon	1598			33° 28.00' N	118° 32.00' W
a Marta	Galleon	1582			33° 28.00' N	118° 30.00' W
fic		1951			33° 29.00' N	119° 01.00' W
eror	Oil screw	1932	Foundered	56	33° 29.00' N	119° 02.00' W

Big hulls make for awe inspiring dives.

Chapter 11
San Clemente Island

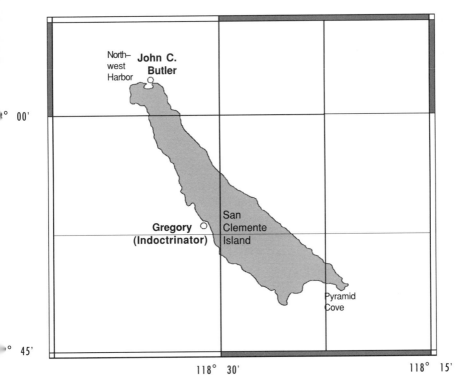

San Clemente Island is a fascinating place. It is the farthest South of the offshore
~ds in Southern California. San Clemente Island is owned and operated by the United
~s Navy. As a training location, the Navy uses San Clemente island for live fire exercises
~val artillery, bombs and missiles at the island to keep their skills sharp. They may close
~sland at any time for any reason, so pay attention to their requests at all times. You do
~vant to stagger into the path of an incoming tomahawk cruise missile or F-18 bomb-
~in.

John C. Butler

The John C. Butler is a famous ship. It was a DE or Destroyer Escort built du
WWII as about the smallest practical fighting ship possible. They were only 300 feet l
and displaced a mere 1350 tons, and originally intended to provide convoy defense aga
submarines. Not only did they perform admirably in this role, but the DEs and t
crews distinguished themselves time and time again even when finding themselves con
up against overwhelmingly superior firepower. They fought on and won battles solely
the skill of their captains and bravery of their crews. Imagine a 1300 ton DE with its p
3 and 5 inch guns slugging it out with 75,000 ton Japanese battlewagons with 18 inch g
capable of hurling over a ton of high explosives nearly 30 miles. This mismatch is so
thing akin to a Chihuahua squaring off against a Kodiak bear - AND WINNING!
hard to comprehend the sheer guts it took to defend our nation against some of the n
terrifying pyrotechnic capabilities of all time, especially such confrontations as
granddaddy of all ship to ship Naval battles of all time, the battle of Leyte Gulf.

The John C. Butler's keel was laid down in Texas in October of 1943. By Au
1944, the DE was in harms way, participating in pre-invasion strikes of the island
Morotai and Pelilu in the Philippines. Next, the John C. Butler was sailing as air defense
the carrier groups making for Leyte Gulf. When the battle broke out, massive battle
and cruiser shells were flying everywhere. The DE's were launching torpedos, firing
cannons and dodging whatever was being aimed at them as the battle raged for hou
the darkness. When dawn broke and the smoke had cleared, the back of the Japa
Navy had been broken. They were never again able to mount an offensive attack on
American naval fleet.

The war wasn't over for the Butler just yet. The ship had to fight off kama
attacks in later battles to retake the Philippines, and participated in several other cr
Pacific island battles, Iwo Jima and Okinawa. There, it had the most dangerous ship
of the war, outer picket patrol, to serve as bait for the fearsome kamikaze attacks.
brave crew and gallant ship came through, beating back numerous suicide attacks. Or
20th of May 1945, the ship was attacked by six kamikaze planes from Okinawa. It spla
five of them but one struck the ship and caused only minor damage to the superstruc
and antennas.

The Butler was decommissioned after the war but was brought out of mothball
the Korean war in 1950 and was again decommissioned in 1957. It was taken to San Clem

*The John C, Butler, after helping win the biggest and most decisive Naval battle in history, the
Battle of Leyte Gulf, steams for Iwo Jima, the bloody island campaign where Japan's fate was
sealed, securing an airfield within striking distance to the home islands.*

...nd in 1970 where it was used as a bombing target. Even then, the old veteran refused ...give up after being struck with several bombs in practice runs at sea. It was towed into ...rthwest Anchorage of San Clemente Island and used as a training exercise for Navy ...ALs underwater demolitions teams (UDTs). They blew the ship up in a training exer-... and it finally sank to the bottom of the anchorage. Several times since, it has been used ...a SEAL training tool and UDTs have set off charges blowing the ship into several ...ces as it lies at the bottom. It lies at:

33° 02.166'N x 118° 34.916'W

Because the Butler is inside the anchorage at Northwest harbor, San Clemente Is-
...l, it rarely gets fished. Occasionally, fishermen holed up in Northwest Anchorage wait-
...for weather to clear, descover thet the Butler is an excellent place to fish and manage to
...up big Sheepshead and other reef species. In addition, plenty of lobsters live here. It's
...ays worth a stop.

Divers say that spending time with the old warhorse in its final resting site is almost
...iritual experience. The John C. Butler sits upright on a sandy bottom. The bow was
...vn off and now sits in deeper water. About 60' of the mid-section remains intact.
...out 50 yards aft of the main section lies one of the ship's 5 inch guns. The depth charge
...s, fantail and propellers are also visible and fairly intact. Much of the metal is jagged
...sharp, so days with reduced visibility and surge currents can make this a dangerous
...eavor. The contrast between the hull and the white sand bottom make this wreck a
...t place for photography.

...gory (Indoctrinator)

Another WWII vetran,
...destroyer Gregory, DD-
...was launched in Tacoma
...hington in May of 1944
...in the war in the Pacific.
...first shots the ship fired
...ger were at the bloody
...e for Iwo Jima. The Gre-
...was in close, offering the
...nes on the ground close
...upport. As the battle was
...ing down, the destroyer
...l for Saipan to prepare
...he Okinawa invasion.
...8, 1945 found the Gre-
...participating in a diver-
...ary strike against the
...east coast of Okinawa,
...ft attention from the real
...ng occuring on the West-

Big bull Sheepshead, like this 20 pounder, are denizens of artificial reefs and wrecks, and are highly sought after for their excellent table fare.

ern coast. The diversion worked and attracted the Japanese defensive strikes. The prim
Japanese anti-ship weapons at that time were kamikaze strikes. Three suicide aircraft
tacked the Gregory at sunset. The ships gunners riddled them with machine gun f
demolishing all three. One of the shot up suicide planes, wingless and with the pilot de
managed to spiral into the broadside of the ship causing substantial damage. The s
sailed back to San Diego for repairs but the war ended and the ship was decomissio
after the war.

When the Korean war broke out the Gregory was again recommissioned and s
into the fray. The ship was a participant in the Korean war, both shelling land targets a
being shot at often from shore batteries. After the war, the ship continued its Naval po
projection role until 1964 when it was finally retired and renamed the Indoctrinator, to
used as a non-operational training ship for Navy recruits in San Diego. In 1972 the s
was towed out near San Clemente Island where it was used as a bombing target, t
finally towed to its present location and used to train Navy SEAL UDT teams. It is
occasionally used by the Navy for underwater demolitions training. It lies scattered al
the surf line in water up to about 30 feet deep at:

32° 53.083'N x 118° 31.083'W

The Gregory gets plenty of kelp growing on its structure, when Navy SEALS ar
blowing it up, and so attracts surface fish galore. In the spring, it is a great attracto
White Seabass, and in the warmer weather, Yellowtail are a common sight here. Man
overnight island partyboat has saved the trip by stopping here to load up on Yello
when some of the other popular spots at San Clemente Island aren't producing. In a
tion to the big game fish found here, it is also a great spot for reef fish: Perch and C
Bass. In all, the Indoctrinator is one of the best all round fishing holes on the island.

*The Gregory steaming off Okinawa during WWII before being hit bt a
kamikaze plane*

ter here can be rough, though, and tricky currents pass the weather face of San Clemente
nd. Also, make sure you're not out there when the Navy is using this area for training,
keep tabs on the NOTMs if you plan to fish this productive spot.

Because of the Gregory's position, in shallow water on the exposed weather side of
Clemente Island, the wreck can only be dived on when you have a combination of
factors. The first is when the Navy permits boating or diving operations on the site,
en no exercises are planned, and second, when the weather and seas are calm. The
ge and currents can be brutal and visibility poor, but when things calm down, the
ck can provide a fascinating dive. The ship is fairly complete and much of the guns,
chinery, fittings and hull pieces are readily recognizable.

exploded Ordinance near San Clemente Island

Beware anywhere around San Clemente Island, including underwater. The Navy has
n shelling and bombing the island for many years and who knows how much
xploded ordinance might still be scattered along the bottom. If you're not sure what it
t is strongly recommended that you leave it alone.

litional Wrecks around San Clemente Island

Following is the database for wrecks in this area. They're arranged from North to
th by wreck location:

Name	Type	Sunk	Reason	Tons	Coordinates	
San Clemente Island						
a Rosa	Galleon	1717			32° 25.00' N	119° 06.00' W
land	Bark	1901	Capsized		32° 37.02' N	119° 07.08' W
sden	Destroyer escort	1975			32° 47.00' N	118° 42.00' W
nde		1941			32° 48.00' N	118° 20.00' W
		1949			32° 48.00' N	118° 25.00' W
Gabriel	Oil screw	1931		39	32° 48.00' N	118° 23.00' W
s	Destroyer	1976			32° 48.00' N	118° 24.00' W
ncia	Oil screw	1933	Burned	60	32° 49.00' N	118° 23.00' W
rican Beauty		1954			32° 50.00' N	118° 25.00' W
a Domingo	Galleon	1540			32° 50.00' N	118° 18.00' W
fish	Submarine	1969			32° 53.00' N	118° 36.00' W
ory	Destroyer escort	1972	demolition	2050	32° 53.08' N	118° 31.05' W
		1937			32° 54.05' N	118° 30.00' W
ack		1951			32° 55.00' N	118° 34.00' W
y	Submarine	1970			32° 59.00' N	118° 32.00' W
nt	Oil screw	1965			33° 00.00' N	118° 31.00' W
1 455	Landing craft	1956			33° 00.00' N	118° 35.00' W
C Butler	Destroyer escort	1970	Used as target		33° 02.17' N	118° 34.92' W
vieve H II	Oil screw	1956		112	33° 10.00' N	118° 30.00' W

The bright orange Garabaldi - California's state fish. It is illegal to take these plentiful reef fish. Their agressive nature makes them often hilarious to watch as they go about their business as denizens of the reef.

Chapter 12
Yet Another Wreck Database

Just when you were thinking, "It just doesn't get any better than this," it does! There
another fascinating resource for the undersea explorer, one that'll make every adventurer's
od pump a bit faster.

The National Oceanographic and Atmospheric Administration, those wonderful
s who are responsible for printing up Nautical Charts, has begun an intensive mapping
well traveled shipping and boating routes, with some very sophisticated high tech, side
aning sonar, with the intention to locate any submerged objects that may pose a hazard
avigation. That means divable depths. This survey is being performed by the Office

Coast Survey's
t o m a t e d
ck and Ob-
ction Infor-
ion System
OIS) and
r database
ains informa-
on approxi-
ly 10,000 sub-
ged wrecks
obstructions
e coastal wa-
of the United
s. I've sepa-
out the part
eir huge da-
se that applies

Diving objects from the AWOIS database is like a box of chocolates....
(Well, you know the rest.)

to Southern California.

Most of the shipwrecks in this database are unknown, yet there are very accurate a
precise coordinates for each target. What are they? Well, you never know. This database
assembled using the latest in bottom imaging technology to discover anything in the wa
that could possibly be a hazard to navigation - and I mean anything - old pickup truc
sunken small boats, shipping containers that may have accidentally slipped off the dec
of ships, contraband freight that intentionally went over one side as customs offici
climbed up the other, and just maybe, old Spanish galleons or Russian pirate ships, stuf
with gold and jewels sitting there just waiting for a weekend diver to glide by and disco
the treasure.

Some of these targets within the confines of LA Harbor are in an area of the in
harbor where people used to anchor their old boats when they got tired of paying
fees every month. The boats would eventually disappear, either slowly as poor mair
nance and winter storms gradually filled them with seawater, or sometimes quickly, wh
a few tweaks of a through hull fitting by the owner, hastening the reduction of
unfinished, over budget project, into a mere bad memory.

Whatever and wherever, have fun with it - and if you discover treasure, please o
the author a finder's fee, or at least let him know what the obstruction actually is, for
next book revision.

Description	Depth	Coordinates	
LOUISA		34° 52.399'	120° 42.560'
I.G.KULUKUNDIS		34° 39.299'	120° 37.360'
UNKNOWN		34° 36.999'	120° 37.560'
CGC MCCULLOCH		34° 29.299'	120° 29.560'
OBSTRUCTION	4.1	34° 28.043'	120° 12.387'
OBSTRUCTION		34° 27.144'	120° 08.890'
BERKLEY		34° 26.999'	120° 36.360'
BRANT		34° 26.807'	120° 01.232'
OBSTRUCTION		34° 26.659'	120° 16.388'
OBSTRUCTION		34° 26.641'	120° 28.173'
OBSTRUCTION		34° 26.624'	120° 13.022'
OBSTRUCTION		34° 26.383'	120° 13.709'
OBSTRUCTION		34° 26.341'	120° 13.017'
OBSTRUCTION		34° 26.266'	120° 23.359'
OBSTRUCTION		34° 26.249'	120° 23.076'
OBSTRUCTION		34° 26.216'	120° 14.009'
OBSTRUCTION		34° 26.208'	120° 11.476'
OBSTRUCTION	9.1	34° 26.130'	120° 23.422'
OBSTRUCTION		34° 26.116'	120° 09.275'
OBSTRUCTION		34° 26.116'	120° 23.209'
OBSTRUCTION		34° 26.099'	120° 08.675'
OBSTRUCTION		34° 26.099'	120° 23.326'

OBSTRUCTION		34° 26.083'	120° 10.292'
OBSTRUCTION		34° 26.083'	120° 10.825'
OBSTRUCTION		34° 26.083'	120° 23.243'
OBSTRUCTION		34° 26.066'	120° 09.625'
OBSTRUCTION		34° 26.066'	120° 23.443'
OBSTRUCTION		34° 25.983'	120° 23.276'
OBSTRUCTION		34° 25.966'	120° 23.393'
OBSTRUCTION		34° 25.933'	120° 07.825'
OBSTRUCTION		34° 25.933'	120° 23.359'
OBSTRUCTION		34° 25.916'	120° 09.775'
OBSTRUCTION		34° 25.911'	120° 22.655'
OBSTRUCTION		34° 25.899'	120° 21.526'
OBSTRUCTION		34° 25.899'	120° 22.426'
OBSTRUCTION		34° 25.899'	120° 23.143'
OBSTRUCTION		34° 25.833'	120° 22.543'
OBSTRUCTION		34° 25.799'	120° 22.959'
OBSTRUCTION		34° 25.783'	120° 22.576'
OBSTRUCTION		34° 25.766'	120° 23.343'
OBSTRUCTION		34° 25.733'	120° 08.209'
OBSTRUCTION		34° 25.733'	120° 22.609'
OBSTRUCTION		34° 25.716'	120° 22.659'
OBSTRUCTION		34° 25.683'	120° 22.859'
OBSTRUCTION	2.9	34° 25.670'	119° 54.990'
OBSTRUCTION	4.1	34° 25.666'	119° 55.201'
OBSTRUCTION	1.9	34° 25.632'	119° 54.817'
OBSTRUCTION	5.2	34° 25.630'	119° 55.362'
OBSTRUCTION		34° 25.616'	120° 23.226'
OBSTRUCTION		34° 25.516'	120° 28.126'
OBSTRUCTION	4.2	34° 25.485'	119° 55.092'
OBSTRUCTION	5.7	34° 25.479'	119° 54.985'
OBSTRUCTION	5.3	34° 25.462'	119° 54.704'
OBSTRUCTION	1.1	34° 25.456'	119° 54.503'
OBSTRUCTION		34° 25.432'	119° 54.449'
OBSTRUCTION		34° 25.426'	119° 54.639'
OBSTRUCTION		34° 25.386'	119° 54.391'
OBSTRUCTION		34° 25.343'	119° 54.328'
OBSTRUCTION		34° 25.308'	119° 54.250'
OBSTRUCTION		34° 25.266'	119° 54.183'
OBSTRUCTION		34° 25.225'	119° 54.120'
OBSTRUCTION	0.1	34° 25.216'	119° 53.886'
OBSTRUCTION		34° 25.180'	119° 53.633'
OBSTRUCTION		34° 25.033'	119° 53.333'
OBSTRUCTION		34° 24.399'	120° 20.559'
OBSTRUCTION	2.2	34° 24.272'	119° 52.698'
OBSTRUCTION	3.1	34° 24.185'	119° 50.470'
OBSTRUCTION	2.9	34° 24.179'	119° 50.500'
OBSTRUCTION	14.3	34° 24.098'	119° 49.512'
OBSTRUCTION		34° 23.666'	119° 55.558'
OBSTRUCTION		34° 23.266'	119° 53.875'
TENACIOUS		34° 23.000'	119° 53.058'

JANE STANFORD		34° 23.000'	119° 41.058'
OBSTRUCTION		34° 22.816'	119° 52.325'
OBSTRUCTION		34° 22.783'	119° 52.058'
OBSTRUCTION		34° 22.683'	119° 51.808'
UNKNOWN		34° 18.499'	120° 45.960'
UNKNOWN		34° 14.620'	119° 16.623'
UNKNOWN		34° 14.620'	122° 16.633'
UNKNOWN		34° 14.550'	119° 16.947'
UNKNOWN		34° 14.545'	122° 16.953'
OBSTRUCTION		34° 09.315'	119° 16.064'
UNKNOWN		34° 08.650'	119° 14.000'
LA JENELLE (NORTH)		34° 08.093'	119° 17.731'
LA JENELLE (SOUTH)		34° 07.743'	119° 17.784'
OUTFALL		34° 07.486'	119° 11.918'
PIPELINE	20	34° 07.403'	119° 10.535'
PLATFORM - GINA		34° 07.041'	119° 16.657'
CABLE AREA		34° 05.860'	119° 13.151'
UNKNOWN		34° 04.000'	119° 08.556'
AMAZON		34° 02.001'	119° 00.056'
REAPER		34° 01.150'	119° 32.307'
SAN FRANCISCO		34° 01.000'	119° 19.557'
STAR OF HOLLYWOOD		33° 59.801'	118° 31.255'
SAN GIUSEPPE		33° 56.000'	119° 22.057'
UNKNOWN		33° 54.205'	120° 08.338'
CHICKASAW		33° 54.000'	120° 07.775'
UNKNOWN		33° 51.001'	118° 30.055'
PAN PACIFIC		33° 46.751'	119° 10.390'
SOUNDING	1.1	33° 46.601'	118° 14.554'
UNKNOWN		33° 46.592'	118° 14.515'
UNKNOWN	0.6	33° 46.349'	118° 14.878'
OBSTRUCTION		33° 46.334'	118° 14.914'
OBSTRUCTION	0	33° 46.329'	118° 14.928'
SOUNDING	0	33° 46.318'	118° 14.904'
OBSTRUCTION		33° 46.208'	118° 15.000'
OBSTRUCTION	0	33° 46.141'	118° 14.024'
OBSTRUCTION		33° 45.973'	118° 15.178'
OBSTRUCTION		33° 45.894'	118° 13.315'
OBSTRUCTION		33° 45.883'	118° 14.519'
UNKNOWN	1.4	33° 45.818'	118° 15.418'
UNKNOWN	0	33° 45.751'	118° 15.454'
OBSTRUCTION		33° 45.737'	118° 15.981'
UNKNOWN		33° 45.634'	118° 10.721'
UNKNOWN	13	33° 45.603'	118° 15.436'
UNKNOWN		33° 45.335'	118° 11.771'
OBSTRUCTION		33° 45.314'	118° 16.655'
OBSTRUCTION		33° 45.305'	118° 13.813'
OBSTRUCTION	0	33° 45.301'	118° 17.088'
OBSTRUCTION	0	33° 45.291'	118° 16.646'
UNKNOWN		33° 45.285'	118° 11.571'
OBSTRUCTION		33° 45.282'	118° 16.860'

OBSTRUCTION		33° 45.278'	118° 13.915'
OBSTRUCTION	0	33° 45.260'	118° 16.580'
OBSTRUCTION	10.7	33° 45.228'	118° 13.949'
OBSTRUCTION		33° 45.206'	118° 13.572'
OBSTRUCTION	0	33° 45.193'	118° 16.423'
OBSTRUCTION		33° 45.136'	118° 13.687'
OBSTRUCTION		33° 45.105'	118° 13.786'
UNKNOWN	1	33° 45.098'	118° 14.509'
OBSTRUCTION	0	33° 45.051'	118° 14.704'
OBSTRUCTION	0	33° 45.013'	118° 14.831'
ANDREW D	0	33° 45.001'	118° 50.055'
SOUTHLAND	0	33° 45.001'	119° 25.057'
OBSTRUCTION		33° 44.959'	118° 16.425'
UNKNOWN		33° 44.935'	118° 11.304'
OBSTRUCTION		33° 44.899'	118° 16.452'
UNKNOWN		33° 44.896'	118° 08.832'
OBSTRUCTION	29	33° 44.751'	118° 13.304'
UNKNOWN	0	33° 44.719'	118° 15.219'
OBSTRUCTION	2.6	33° 44.706'	118° 14.311'
UNKNOWN	0	33° 44.611'	118° 16.594'
UNKNOWN	2	33° 44.591'	118° 14.664'
OBSTRUCTIONS	0	33° 44.568'	118° 14.004'
OBSTRUCTION		33° 44.418'	118° 13.754'
UNKNOWN		33° 44.351'	118° 14.394'
UNKNOWN		33° 44.235'	118° 15.988'
OBSTRUCTION		33° 44.218'	118° 16.154'
UNKNOWN		33° 44.201'	118° 16.188'
UNKNOWN		33° 44.060'	118° 16.013'
PHILIPPINE	0	33° 44.001'	118° 15.054'
PIERPOINT QUE	0	33° 43.601'	118° 11.754'
FOX	0	33° 43.584'	118° 08.637'
CITY OF LONG BEACH		33° 43.434'	118° 10.237'
UNKNOWN		33° 42.918'	118° 13.471'
OBSTRUCTION		33° 42.910'	118° 16.617'
SEA PRINCE	0	33° 42.751'	118° 15.638'
UNKNOWN		33° 42.661'	118° 14.464'
SOUTHERN EXPLORER		33° 42.601'	118° 14.664'
OBSTRUCTION		33° 42.600'	118° 16.650'
UNKNOWN		33° 42.593'	118° 16.745'
OBSTRUCTION		33° 42.516'	118° 15.088'
OBSTRUCTION		33° 42.510'	118° 15.107'
UNKNOWN	0	33° 42.501'	118° 15.054'
BAHADA	0	33° 42.501'	118° 15.054'
OBSTRUCTION	0	33° 42.434'	118° 09.204'
DISCOVERY		33° 42.383'	118° 15.067'
LOOP	52	33° 41.910'	118° 16.038'
UNKNOWN	0	33° 41.885'	118° 16.054'
OBSTRUCTION	0	33° 41.401'	118° 15.554'
OBSTRUCTION		33° 40.568'	118° 13.671'
OBSTRUCTION		33° 40.451'	118° 13.338'

ST. JAMES	0	33° 39.401'	118° 21.054'
OLYMPIC II	0	33° 39.401'	118° 13.804'
OLYMPIC	0	33° 39.401'	118° 13.854'
ACE ONE	0	33° 38.835'	118° 11.887'
UNKNOWN	0	33° 37.512'	117° 59.892'
SANTA CECILIA	0	33° 30.002'	118° 27.055'
DIXIE	0	33° 23.902'	118° 22.054'
WESTERN PILOT	0	33° 22.002'	117° 45.053'
OBSTRUCTION	0	33° 20.852'	118° 19.138'
AMER ROSE	0	33° 17.002'	118° 54.556'
UNKNOWN	0	33° 12.002'	117° 54.053'
UNKNOWN	0	33° 02.169'	118° 34.972'
LOS ANGELOS	0	33° 00.002'	120° 00.057'
OBSTRUCTION	0	32° 48.252'	118° 22.554'
OBSTRUCTION	0	32° 43.836'	117° 38.220'
UNKNOWN	0	32° 43.686'	117° 12.719'
OBSTRUCTION		32° 43.330'	117° 12.911'
OBSTRUCTION		32° 42.846'	117° 12.523'
UNKNOWN		32° 42.497'	117° 13.885'
OBSTRUCTION		32° 42.456'	117° 10.230'
UNKNOWN		32° 42.225'	117° 10.488'
UNKNOWN		32° 42.093'	117° 10.282'
UNKNOWN	5	32° 41.959'	117° 10.094'
UNKNOWN	0	32° 41.836'	117° 09.202'
UNKNOWN	0	32° 41.420'	117° 14.352'
OBSTRUCTION		32° 41.273'	117° 13.677'
OBSTRUCTION		32° 41.205'	117° 13.725'
OBSTRUCTION	0	32° 41.202'	117° 13.667'
OBSTRUCTION		32° 41.200'	117° 13.675'
OBSTRUCTION		32° 41.037'	117° 07.752'
UNKNOWN		32° 40.725'	117° 13.955'
OBSTRUCTION	0	32° 40.320'	117° 08.035'
CALIFORNIA	0	32° 40.003'	117° 13.952'
UNKNOWN		32° 39.803'	117° 14.052'
UNKNOWN		32° 39.653'	117° 07.942'
UNKNOWN		32° 39.518'	117° 13.712'
UNKNOWN		32° 39.513'	117° 07.720'
UNKNOWN		32° 39.437'	117° 14.452'
UNKNOWN		32° 39.420'	117° 09.019'
UNKNOWN		32° 39.170'	117° 08.835'
ZARCO		32° 39.153'	117° 30.053'
UNKNOWN		32° 39.117'	117° 12.050'
OBSTRUCTION		32° 38.837'	117° 09.452'
OBSTRUCTION		32° 38.720'	117° 14.169'
UNKNOWN		32° 38.544'	117° 07.260'
UNKNOWN		32° 38.420'	117° 07.368'
UNKNOWN		32° 38.280'	117° 07.430'
UNKNOWN		32° 38.013'	117° 06.989'
OBSTRUCTION	8	32° 37.822'	117° 06.605'
UNKNOWN		32° 37.703'	117° 06.552'

UNKNOWN	27	32° 37.646'	117° 15.115'
UNKNOWN		32° 37.553	117° 14.285'
UNKNOWN		32° 36.720'	117° 06.718'
UNKNOWN		32° 36.553'	117° 07.335'
UNKNOWN		32° 36.470'	117° 06.785'
UNKNOWN		32° 36.303	117° 08.235'
OBSTRUCTION		32° 35.503'	117° 11.052'
OBSTRUCTION		32° 32.703'	117° 15.452'
OBSTRUCTION		32° 32.170'	117° 12.552'
LSIL 837		32° 32.000'	117° 46.053'
OBSTRUCTION		32° 32 170'	117° 14.052'
OBSTRUCTION		32° 31.000'	117° 12.052'
OBSTRUCTION		32° 30.000'	117° 12.052'
SANTA ROSA		32° 27.000'	119° 07.555'
UNKNOWN		32° 26.254'	117° 08.552'
MOLOKAI		31° 50.001'	116° 38.051'
D.T.B NO.16 35		31° 35.340'	116° 00.932'
WESTGATE		31° 30.001'	117° 30.052'

Sometimes the sea so erodes wrecks, you're not sure just what you're looking at

Chapter 13
Teasure Galleons

No book about shipwrecks would be complete without stories of lost galleons, ... es, and treasure chests brimming with jewels and gold doubloons. Well, Southern ... fornia has its share, and very likely, as new technologies are being developed, some of ... e lost treasures may be discovered.

When Columbus sailed into the great ocean sea and discovered America, he thought ... as headed for China. China was very important to Europe in the Middle Ages for ... trade goods. China was the primary source of spices, silk and fancy porcelain, still ... d "china" to this day. Spices in renaissance Europe weren't just used by housewives to ... it up a notch, (BAM!) for their evening meals. Spices were a preservative method for ... s. Remember, there were no freezers, refrigerators, or even ice for iceboxes, then. ... : quickly spoiled in the warm summers heat. Drying, smoking, salting and yes, spicing ... all methods used to preserve meats and keep them from spoiling.

Aside from wool, the fabrics made in Europe were mostly flax based linens. While ... "in" now to wear linen, much of the cloth was more crude in those days, and the ... al work clothes worn by peasants were more like burlap, than what you think of as ... ern linen fabrics. The wealthy of Europe much preferred the vibrant colors and ... c feel of silk fabrics, only available from China at the time.

All Chinese trade goods had to come to Europe by means of a long journey lasting ... hs, or even years, across the continent of Asia, on the backs of pack animals. Much ... is cargo was hijacked by bandits along the way, making the arduous journey expen- ... and risk laden. Shipment by ship was much less expensive in both direct costs of ... , and the costs of lost goods along the way, even factoring in the dangers of ocean ... at the time. When the King and Queen of Spain sent Columbus out with three ships

to discover a trade route, they didn't do it to be altruistic or in the spirit of adventure
did it to get rich.

By the mid 1500s, Spain had established colonies in the new world and in the P
pines. In 1565, the first of a series of treasure voyages sailed from Manila harbor i
Philippines bound for Acapulco, crammed to the gunwales with Chinese trade good
Acapulco, the goods were packed across Mexico to Veracruz, where they were
loaded on Spanish ships bound for Europe, along with new world treasures of gol
silver. The Manila galleons then sailed back across the Pacific with gold and silver, to
up on yet more Chinese goods. The journey from Acapulco to Manila was usually
pleasant, the easterly trade winds gently urged the old ships along in a mostly mild we
tropical path. Returning from Manila to Acapulco, though, ships had to sail North in
wilder North Pacific to take advantage of the prevailing Westerlies, making the retur
far more dangerous than the outbound. It was a six month long, grueling passage
bad weather, pirates and dangerous waters, particularly in Southern California. Fo
years, from 1565 to 1815, the Manila galleons kept up their circular shipping route,
ing Chinese riches to Europe via the long route.

More than 12 of these ships has been known to disappear into the sea, laden
wealth and treasures, worth today, in the hundreds of millions of dollars. Many think
distant memories of the past are gone forever, yet it is only now, in the late 20th and
21st century that the technology has even made locating these ships possible.

As an example of these ships being lost for eons, the Nuestra Senora de la Conce
left from Manila bound for Acapulco. She was wrecked on the southwest tip of the i
of Saipan, Sept. 20, 1638. She was the largest of the Spanish Manila galleons at
displacing about 2,000 tons. An American by the name of William Mathers locate
wreck in 1987. He has since salvaged many priceless treasures from the site. Yet an
ship, the San Diego, sank right in Manila Bay, yet was only discovered in 1991. It is
ently being excavated by divers, and has yielded over 28,000 items to date. It was
when a Manila Galleon called the San Agustin, lost in 1594, was discovered right o
of Drakes Bay in Northern California.

Some of the Manila Galleons that may still reside in or near Southern Cali
include:

Santa Marta

The Santa Marta was a Manila galleon on its return trip from Manila to Acapul
1582 it ran aground, reportedly at Catalina Island. The crew made it to the island
probably some of the cargo also. where it was buried. Most of the cargo was likely
An estimated two hundred tons of Far East treasures disappeared with the ship. Th
no record on any attempts to salvage the cargo at the time, however, the location o
wreck was known then. The remains of the cargo could be worth millions today
possible some or all of the cargo could have been salvaged in the past 420 years, b
one knows for sure. The reported position is:

33° 28' N x 118° 30' W

estra Senora de Ayuda

The Nuestra Senora de Ayuda was 320 tons, also returning to Mexico from Manila h a load of Chinese treasures in 1641. The ship supposedly struck a rock near Catalina, sunk. Some crew managed to make it ashore but all of the cargo was lost. There was record of any salvage attempts. Some insist this ship struck a boiler rock near Santa a Island, not Catalina. It's official reported position is:

33° 26' N x 118° 35' W

Sebastian

The San Sebastian was an outbound Manila Galleon, headed toward the Philippines 754 with a load of gold and silver bullion to be traded for Chinese goods. Spotted by English pirate George Compton on Jan. 7, the ship was forced aground on a rock :rop just west of Santa Catalina Island. The ship sank in about 170' of water. Twenty of the crewmen managed to make it to the island, but they were hunted down by npton's men and killed. The entirety of the cargo was lost. The reported position of San Sebastian is:

33° 18' N x 118° 30' W

Pedro

Another Manila Galleon lost near Santa Catalina Island. Few details of the loss of ship are known, but substantial cargo was lost with the ship. It's reported position is:

33° 28' N x 118° 32' W

o Domingo

The Santo Domingo was lost near San Clemente Island, reported at:

32 50' N x 118 18' W.

In addition to the Manila Galleons, California had its wild west days during the Gold from 1849 until the 1860s, when there was plenty of gold transported down the by ship. A number of high profile cargos were lost at sea and never recovered. It's mpossible that stacks of gold bars are today lying in a heap on the bottom of the just waiting for a lucky diver to swim by. A few of these wrecks include:

ee Blade

This shipwreck is discussed in detail in Chapter 3, Santa Barbara and Ventura County. Yankee Blade was lost at Point Pedernales in 1854 carrying a cargo of gold bullion the rich gold strikes in Northern California.. The shipwreck has been located and red, but a considerable controversy rages over whether all of cargo had been recov- See the Santa Barbara section for the wreck location.

ield Scott:

This ship also had a considerable amount of treasure aboard when it crashed into the Northern shore of Anacapa Island in 1853. It has been mostly salvaged, however i not known if all of the gold bars were all ever recovered. Of course this ship is now in National Marine Sanctuary of the Channel Islands so is a "cultural resource," and may be disturbed. See the Channel Islands section for its location.

Some Additional 1850s Era Shipwrecks

Eliza Thornton	1856	Santa Barbara	34° 24'45'N 119° 41'00'W
Mazzani	1856	Santa Barbara	34° 24'45'N 119° 41'00'W
Pilgram	1852	Los Angeles	33° 55'00'N 118° 50'00'W
Plutus	1858	San Diego	32° 39'45'N 117° 14'30'W
Lovely Flora	1858	San Diego	32° 40'00'N 117° 15'00'W

It is unknown if any of these ships had any valuable cargo or if the cargo was recovered.

Wine, anyone?

Chapter 14
Artificial Reef and Wreck Fish

Certain species of fish are commonly caught in and around reefs and wrecks in
thern California. There are three primary types. Reef dwellers that actually spend their
in and around the reefs, flats dwellers that are attracted to the reefs because of the
idance of life there but live in the sandy or muddy bottoms surrounding the reefs and
ks, and finally free swimming surface fish who pass by the reefs only to dine. This
ter lists the most common of these three types of fish you'll likely encounter when
ng or diving these areas. Don't take this to mean these are the only fish you'll find here
re are literally dozens of other species that are possible to catch in these habitats - these
ust the most common.

In addition to fish, the reef diver will encounter countless varieties of sea anemones,
ish, crabs, lobsters, clams, limpets, scallops, mussels, barnacles, sea cucumbers, and
ts of all sorts when visiting shipwrecks and reefs. The enormous variety of life is what
es visiting these places so fascinating, To attempt to catalogue or mention even a few
ie more common plants and animals you might come across could fill volumes in
, so is beyond the scope of this book. Only the major game fish will be discussed.

f Dwellers

The majority of fish you'll likely encounter when fishing or diving shipwrecks and
cial reefs will be reef dwelling fish. This should be no surprise. These fish rely on
r to live both for protection from marauding predators and as convenient places to
There are probably more reef dwelling species of fish in Southern California than
ither types. Since kelp grows on all shallow reefs in California, all kelp dwelling species
h are essentially reef fish.

Calico Bass

A member of the grouper family, Calico Bass are abundant in Southern Califor[n]
They're ambush feeders taking smaller bait fish. Anchovies, Sardines and Queenfish ([H]
ring or Brown Baits) are the mainstay of their diet. They also take a rubber jig, metal jig
swimming plug properly presented. There is a 12 inch minimum size for Calicos. The[y]
excellent eating.

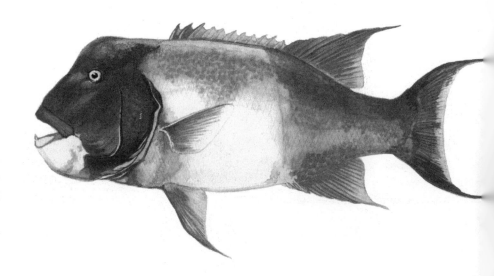

California Sheepshead

Sheepshead are a type of wrasse, a fish that goes through an amazing transition [f]
female to male as they get older. The males can grow as big as 3 feet but most are [n]
smaller. The males are red/black/red banded and the females all red. They feed on shr[imp,]
clams, and other shellfish. They'll hit shrimp, cut squid, or sometimes anchovies, an[d]
also take rubber swim baits and shrimp flies. They're tops as table fare.

Oceanic Whitefish

The Whitefish is a popular Southern California sport fish particularly when not much
is biting. They get up to 3 feet long but fish bigger than about 18 inches are rare.
ey're a greenish color with yellow fins. They're best caught on anchovy or cut squid baits
are very good to eat also.

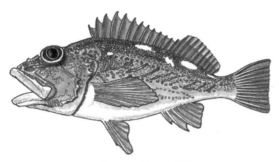

Starry Rockfish

The Starry is a smaller member of the Sebastes (rock fish) family, but still a very
d eating one. They're bright red with star shaped bright white spots. They take ancho-
, cut squid or shrimp flies fished right inside heavy cover. Starries are just one of a wide
ety of different rock fish species

Ling Cod

Moving from their normal deep water haunts where they spend most of the year,
Cod arrive at shallower reefs and wrecks in the late winter and early spring to spawn.
're big, running from 2 to 4 feet long and sometimes in the 40 lb range. They're
ctly adapted for ambushing from heavy cover and will eat live bait from Anchovies
hole Mackerel. They're a dark green and very toothy. The meat can sometimes be a
ish or bluish color, but it cooks up white. They're excellent eating.

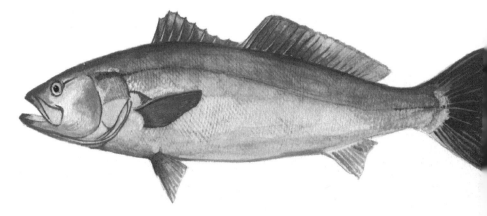

White Seabass

White Seabass aren't bass at all, they're croakers - just like Tomcod, Corbina, and Spotfin and Yellowfin Croakers you might catch in the surf line or off a pier, except course that these croakers get over 6 feet long and over 80 lbs.! White seabass are stag an amazing recovery after gill netting nearly wiped them out, thanks in-part to an excel effort by the United Anglers of Southern California (UASC) and their breeding and gr out program. They're one of the premier game fish of Southern California. They rocky reefs and wrecks and feed primarily on Squid, Sardines and Anchovies. They're t as table fare, also.

Black Seabass

The biggest of the big Southern California reef fish, these monster Groupers been caught weighing over 800 lbs.! They're now protected and stiff fines await poac Recent years have seen more and more numbers of these being caught and release anglers, signaling that the protection measures are working and once again these magnifi giants will prowl local shipwrecks and artificial reefs. They really seem to like shipw: where they can wait in ambush from the intricate cover this type of structure afford you catch one, release it immediately.

Halfmoon

The Halfmoon is a fascinating and plentiful fish in Southern California, They're often
led Blue Perch, though they aren't perch at all. They run in size between 6 or 8 inches, to
er 18 inches, and four pounds. They're good eating and eagerly snap at small cut bait
ey're usually in schools of 20 to 200 or more individual fish. They're called Halfmoons
:ause of the lunate shape of their tails.

Opaleye

Opaleye are often seen around shallow reefs, especially at the islands. They're dark
nish in color with a beautiful opal blue eye color. They're primarily vegetarians, making
n excellent table fare, but will, on occasion, hit bait like cut Squid. Opaleyes are often
e large, getting over 18 inches, but are commonly in the 10-12 inch range.

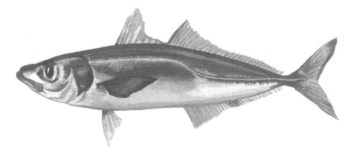

Jack Mackerel

Not really mackerel, Jack Mackerel should really be called "Mackerel Jack" because
're actually Jacks. Other members of the jack family include Yellowtail. Jack Maclerel
excellent table fare though small. You may have ordered them at a sushi bar by the
e Aji.

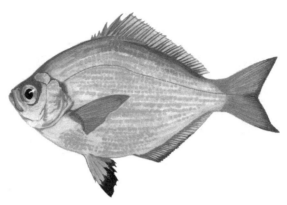

Perch

There are a number of different types of perch living in and around artificial re[...] Of perch in wrecks and reefs, you'll find Walleye Perch, Pile Perch, Rubberlip Perch a[...] several others. All of these fish are good eating but tend to be fairly small. They're cau[...] on cut Squid or small bait catching rigs, usually baited with tiny strips of Anchovy [...] Squid.

Flats Dwellers

Fishes of the sand and mud flats also tend to congregate near shipwrecks and ar[...] cial reefs, simply because that's where the food is. Baitfish seeking shelter, reef fish a[...] bushing prey and leaving scraps behind, and in general, simply more activity in and aro[...] the reefs means that's where the food is. For example the famoug Huntington Flats fish[...] spot is usually thought of as a wide mud flat. It's actually the Bolsa Chica artificial reef v[...] numerous rock piles.

California Halibut

The Halibut is one of the most sought after of the game fish in Southern Califo[...] They patrol the many flats areas around the coast and eagerly take live bait or rubber s[...] baits they come across. They can grow as big as 5 feet and 60 lbs but most are n[...]

naller. There is a 22 inch minimum size in California. They're brownish green on one side d ivory white on the other. Both eyes are on the dark side. They're one of the best eating h in Southern California.

Barred Sand Bass

A very popular game fish in Southern California, Sandies move into the flats areas in late spring and stay most of the summer. They're caught using cut Squid or live Anchos, but will also hit a rubber swim bait. Sand Bass are excellent eating and love the mud l sand bottoms just adjacent to artificial reefs and wrecks. There's a 12 inch minimum e for sand bass also. The world's record fish is a bit over 13 lbs but a 5 pounder is isidered a huge one.

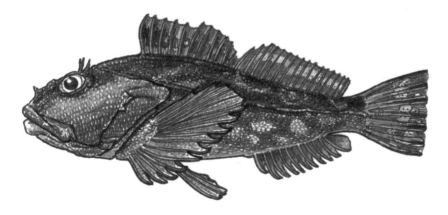

Cabezon

Cabezon are members of the true Sculpin family of fishes and are its largest exle, growing as big as 25 lbs. They're big, ugly and aggressive. They eat Squid or hovies, as well as shellfish, their favorite treat. Cabezon are excellent to eat but, like Cod have a blue-green flesh that's sometimes a turn off to people. Don't worry, the t cooks up white, fluffy and delicious. The roe, however, is poisonous and if eaten can luce violent illness, so be sure you clean them thoroughly if you plan to make a meal of one.

White Croaker

A smaller, very common fish throughout Southern California, the White Croak has been given a bad rap because it's so sensitive to pollution. Signs in many harbors wa fishermen not to eat the fish if caught in the bay and many fishermen take it to me anywhere. The truth is that fish caught in the open ocean are fine to eat, and are in fact qu tasty and healthy. Anyway, White Croaker hit Anchovies and cut Squid readily. They usually 8 to 12 inches long and are very silvery in appearance.

California Scorpionfish (Sculpin)

Sculpin are another favorite of local fishermen - though they're not a Sculpin at they're actually members of the rockfish family, Sebastes. They're usually smaller, run about 10 to 15 inches in length, but are excellent to eat. They have mildly poisonous sp at the base of their fins so should be handled with care. Some people have severe swel when spined by a Sculpin while others just suffer discomfort. They eagerly snap at Squid, shrimp flies, or live Anchovy baits fished right on the bottom. New size limitati are in effect so be sure to get the latest before taking these shallow water bottom dwel

Surface Fish

Plenty of pelagic, free swimming surface fish visit artificial reefs and shipwre again, because that's where the food is. With so many other types of fish in the a including bait fish, can the preditors be far behind?

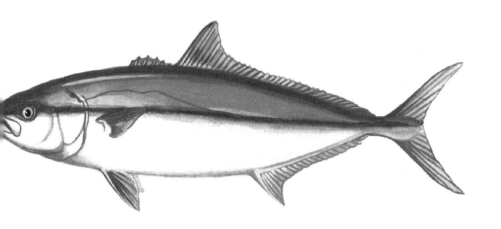

Yellowtail

The premier Southern California game fish, Yellowtail are a fisherman's dream. They're
sometimes over 30 lbs, powerful, fun to fight, and excellent eating. What more could
ask for? They can be caught on live bait - Anchovies, Sardines, live Squid, sometimes
ll Mackerel and on lures of all sorts including rubber swim baits, hard jigs, swimming
gs, and trolled feathers. Home guard Yellowtail can be caught any time of the year, but
warmer summer months bring migratory fish up from Mexico in bigger numbers to
delight of the Southern California angler. Yellowtail have dark green backs and yellow

Bonito

Bonito are not nearly as common as they once were, but are still regularly seen. In
they are making somewhat of a comeback.They hit live bait, shiny jigs, and feather
with equal ease. They're a blast to catch, especially on light tackle since their fight is fast
furious. Bonito are shaped like tuna, are silvery, and have striped markings on their
s. They're good to eat either fresh or smoked.

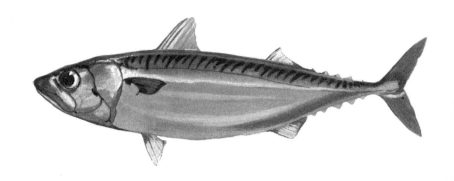

Mackerel

Considered a nuisance by most fishermen, Mackerel are common throughout
California coast. They'll eat almost anything and can be caught using just about any te
nique or tackle in existence. They're green backed with mottled black markings and
grow up to 6 lbs. They're edible but the taste is too strong for many people - most rele
them. They smoke up quite well, though for those who like strong flavored fish. They a
can be prepared sushi-style with salt and vinegar and though aren't quite as good as so
of the Norwegen blue back Mackerel you might find in your local sushi bar, are still a
meal prepared in this manner.

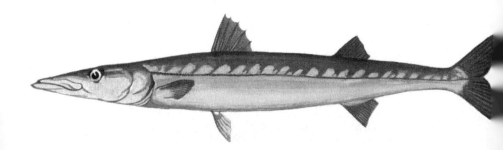

Barracuda

Perhaps the most common Southern California surface game fish, barracuda are
to catch and good to eat. They arrive from mid to late spring in schools and begin cha
bait in a frantic dance of death. By mid summer they slow down a bit and like to p
the mid waters around kelp beds, reefs and wrecks. They can be caught on bait but r
fishermen prefer jigs. Their sharp teeth can cut off a monofilament leader with ease
many on bait are lost. Barracuda run to about 4 feet and 18 lbs. The minimum size ke
in California is 28 inches. They're silvery in color and unmistakable by their shape

Sharks and Rays

There are quite a few types of Sharks and Rays living in Southern California
you're likely to encounter when fishing or diving around artificial reefs and shipwr
Dangerous Sharks are quite rare and tend to hunt in open water, so it's unlikely you'll
into them, but a huge variety of smaller and non-dangerous Sharks makes them a fasc
ing study.

Blue Shark

The most common free swimming Shark in Southern California, Blues are easily ognized by their slender bodies and long fins. While blues can inflict serious injuries, y're not agressive. Blues like more open water but do hunt around the fringes of kelp ls. You may encounter them if diving deeper, open water wrecks. They're not generally isidered edible because of their ammonia tasting flesh and skin, so if you leave them ne, they'll follow suit. Blues can get up to 6 or 8 feet.

Thresher Shark

Threshers are unmistakable for their extra long upper tail fins. Like the Blues, they the potential to cause damage to a swimmer, but tend to avoid anything they don't x is a meal, and that means anything larger than a big Mackerel. Threshers often enter ow water in search of prey and have been caught by surf fishermen. They can grow et long, half of which is their tails Unlike the slender Blue Sharks, Thresher Sharks get bodied and heavier, somtimes several hundred pounds. They're usually caught when ng for other species and are considered very good eating.

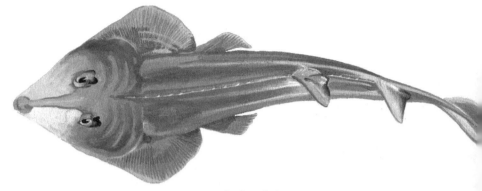

Guitarfish

Often seen probing around sandy bottoms with their snouts, Guitarfish are a v
common sight along shallow sandy bottoms. There are actually two species of this fish
Southern California waters, the Shovelnose (the one pictured) and the Banded, wit
more rounded snout and clearly visible bands of darker brown across the body. The fl
of guitarfish is firm and delicious. They're usually caught using cut strips of fish baits,
mackerel, but will also hit dead anchovies fished right on the bottom.

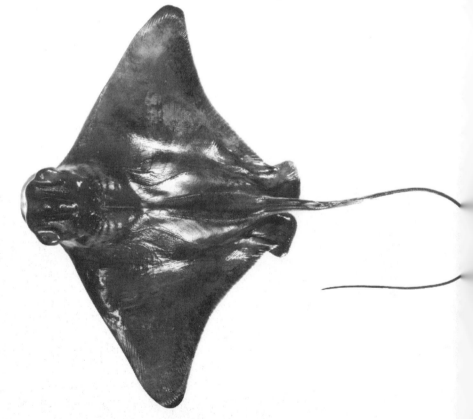

Bat Ray

Though menacing looking, Batrays are essentially harmless when approached ur
water. They grow huge, getting over 6 feet across and weighing several hundred pou

t Rays often inhabit bays and estuaries, so can be quite a shock when encountered in
rky water . Most of the time during the day, though, they're inactive resting buried in
e silt of the bottom, preferring to forage at night.

Sting Rays

California is home to several species of Sting Rays. They can inflict painful wounds
h the stinger at the base of their tails, sometimes mildly toxic. They often lay buried in
sand, with only their eyes showing awaiting prey to swim by and be ambushed. They
ze when approached and even sometimes when touched, but as soon as they feel
iciently threatened, they dash off with a powerful side to side slashing of their tail,
times catching a prodding finger by surprise with their stinging spine.

big Black
bass is an
osng sight
derwater.
ey're now
'ected and
iff fines
ait those
o ignore
'is law.

Chapter 15
Other Resources

There are a number of resources the reef or wreck diver or fishermen should be ~re of and utilize if needed. The organization responsible for the management of fish ~game in California including all fish and game captured in US or International waters landed in the State of California is:

California Department of Fish and Game
1416 Ninth Street
Sacramento, CA 95814
Tel: (916) 445-0411
Fax: (916) 653-1856
Website: http://www.dfg.ca.gov/

The DFG's website includes downloadable documents with all of the regulations, ~ding take limits, minimum sizes, seasons, etc.

If you are planning to SCUBA dive to visit the reefs and wrecks, you should be ~ed and rated for this activity. There are a number of associations offering these train- ~nd rating services including:

PADI Americas
30151 Tomas Street
Rancho Santa Margarita, CA 92688-2125
Tel: (800) 729-7234
Fax: (949) 858 7264
Web: http://www.padi.com/

NAUI Worldwide
PO Box 89789
Tampa, FL 33689-0413
Tel: (800) 553-6284
Fax: (813) 628-8253
Web: http://www.naui.org/

PDIC International
1554 Gardner Avenue
Scranton, PA, 18509, USA
Tel: 717-342-1480
Fax: 717-342-1276
Web: http://www.pdic-intl.com/

Scuba Diving International (SDI)
18 Elm St.
Topsham, ME, 04086, USA
Tel: 207-729-4201
Fax: 207-729-4453
Web: http://www.tdisdi.com/

SSI - Scuba Schools International
2619 Canton Court
Fort Collins, CO, 80525-4498, USA
Tel: 970-482-0883
Fax: 970-482-6157
Web: http://www.ssiusa.com/

YMCA National Scuba Program
101 N. Wacker Drive
Chicago, IL, 60606, USA
Phone: (800) 872-9622
Fax: (312) 977-0894
Web: http://www.ymcascuba.org/

Next, if you are planning to dive on wrecks in California, you should get in con
with the main organization specializing in this activity. The California Wreck Divers a
genuinely great group of men and women dedicated to this fascinating sport. The
members have a wealth of knowledge and are eager to share their knowhow with all
contact them:

California Wreck Divers, Inc.
P.O. Box 10571
Marina Del Rey, CA 90291
Web: http://www.cawreckdivers.org/

Some other important organizations related to shipwrecks of Southern California include:

California State Lands Comission
100 Howe Ave, Suite 100 South
Sacramento, CA 95825-8202
Tel: (916) 574-1900
Fax: (916) 574-1810
Web: http://www.slc.ca.gov/

Submerged Resources Center - National Park Service
2968 Rodeo Park Drive West
Santa Fe, NM 87505
Tel: (505) 988-6750
Fax: (505) 986-5236
Web: http://data2.itc.nps.gov/submerged/

National Oceanographic and Atmospheric Association
14th Street & Constitution Avenue, NW, Room 6217
Washington, D.C. 20230
Tel: (202) 482-6090
Fax: (202) 482-3154
Web: http://www.noaa.gov/

Naval Historical Center
805 Kidder Breese Street SE
Washington Navy Yard, DC 20374-5060
Tel: (202) 433-7880
Fax: (202) 433-7759
Web: http://www.history.navy.mil/

San Diego Oceans Foundation
P.O. Box 90672
San Diego, CA 92169-2672
Tel: (619) 523-1903
Fax: (619) 523-1979
Web: http://www.sdoceans.org/

Los Angeles Maritime Museum
Berth 84, Foot of 6th Street
San Pedro, CA 90731
Tel: (310) 548-7618
Fax: (310) 832-6537
Web: http://www.lamaritimemuseum.org/

Maritime Museum of San Diego
1492 North Harbor Drive
San Diego, CA 92101
Tel: (619) 234-9153
Web: http://www.sdmaritime.com/

Index of Shipwrecks